WHAT EVERY STUDENT SHOULD KNOW ABOUT WRITING ABOUT WORLD LITERATURE

David L. Pike
American University

Longman

Boston Columbus Indianapolis New York San Francisco Upper Saddle River
Amsterdam Cape Town Dubai London Madrid Milan Munich Paris Montreal Toronto
Delhi Mexico City Sao Paulo Sydney Hong Kong Seoul Singapore Taipei Tokyo

Editor-in-Chief: Joseph Terry
Associate Development Editor: Erin Reilly
Executive Marketing Manager: Joyce Nilsen
Senior Supplements Editor: Donna Campion
Production Manager: Donna DeBenedictis
Project Coordination, Text Design, and Electronic Page Makeup: Grapevine Publishing
    Services, Inc.
Copyeditor: Leslie Ballard
Senior Designer: Sue Kinney
Senior Manufacturing Buyer: Roy Pickering
Printer and Binder: R. R. Donnelley-Crawfordsville
Cover Printer: R. R. Donnelley-Crawfordsville

Please visit us at www.pearsonhighered.com

1 2 3 4 5 6 7 8 9 10—DOC—13 12 11 10

Longman
is an imprint of

ISBN 13: 978-0-205-21166-1
ISBN 10:   0-205-21166-6

www.pearsonhighered.com

CONTENTS

PREFACE

"You cannot open a book without learning something."
—Confucius, 551–479 BCE, China

If you are opening this book, you are fortunate indeed, because it means you are enrolled in a course in world literature and will be reading some of the most pleasurable and exciting poems, stories, novels, and plays ever written. You may be less thrilled over the prospect of writing about those poems, stories, novels, and plays, but you should not be. As the essayist Joan Didion asserts, "I write entirely to find out what I'm thinking, what I'm looking at, what I see and what I mean." Writing is one of the most effective ways to make sense of what you are reading, to clarify what doesn't at first make sense, and also to find new ways in which a poem, story, novel, or play continues to complicate the way you see the world. *What Every Student Should Know About Writing About World Literature* is not a writing textbook, but it will provide you with an overview of the types of writing you can expect to be asked to do in your class on world literature.

Writing About World Literature contains eight chapters and two appendices. The first chapter will introduce you to the fundamentals of reading world literature: the ways in which it is similar and the ways in which it differs from your own literature. The following seven chapters provide instruction in and examples of the types of writing and other evaluated work you will be doing in your class: keeping a response journal, participating in class discussion, preparing and giving a class presentation, writing a literary analysis paper, doing research and compiling an annotated bibliography, writing a research paper, and taking an exam. Each chapter includes a student writing sample, many of them based on Nigerian writer Chinua Achebe's short story "Dead Men's Path," to demonstrate how different writing assignments can build on one another. Appendix A provides the basic rules of the MLA Works Cited page and in-text citation; Appendix B gives some brief advice on how to avoid plagiarism in your writing.

1

READING
WORLD LITERATURE

As the publisher Charles Scribner, Jr., put it, "Reading is a means of thinking with another person's mind; it forces you to stretch your own." Many of the things that world literature asks you to think about will be new to you, but the tools you use to stretch your mind to accommodate those thoughts may be surprisingly familiar—you already rely on them every day, and usually without even noticing you are using them. Learning to read effectively opens up the world to you, from Egyptian hieroglyphs to French films, from poems written across the globe to stories set in your own hometown. And reading effectively is the single most important step in the process of learning to write effectively.

Reading Critically

When we read a book for fun, we often find ourselves "reading for the plot" to find out what happened. This is an important and pleasurable form of reading, but it is not an effective way of drawing meaning out of many of the texts you will read in this or any other class on literature. Reading world literature can require greater attention to the cultural context of a specific work of literature and to the fact that it has generally been translated from another language. We will examine those issues, but first, let's take a brief look at some basic strategies for reading any kind of literary writing, as the first step in preparing for class discussion and writing assignments.

Strategies for Reading Critically

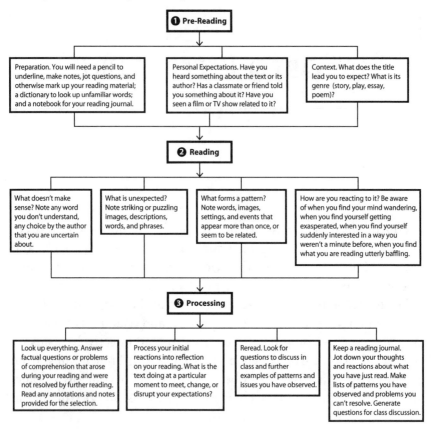

Ambiguity

There are a number of ways in which writing can be ambiguous, or possess multiple potential meanings. Ambiguity can occur on the level of sentence structure, especially in poetry: a word or a phrase that can be read in more than one way. It can occur on the level of setting (where is a particular event taking place?); character (why is a character acting a certain way?); or plot (how are two events related to one another?). Literature often begins by unsettling the reader: plunging us into unfamiliar situations with unfamiliar characters acting in ways we might not immediately understand. But there will always be familiar elements as well, which is where the uncertain sense of ambiguity comes from. Strive to identify what is familiar and what is unfamiliar about any text you are reading.

This will help you pinpoint the important questions and meanings. Most of the time, you should assume that any such ambiguity is intrinsic to the text you are reading and worthy of investigation, rather than a mistake to be dismissed. Although it can sometimes be initially jarring, "strangeness" at all levels of a text is a hallmark of literary writing and one of its most effective tools.

It is important when reading to learn to recognize different forms of ambiguity and to distinguish them from questions of information. The latter questions are the ones you are able to resolve with recourse to a dictionary or a reference source. Question: What is "the meteorite of Anu" (*The Epic of Gilgamesh*, Damrosch and Pike 61, line 99)? Answer: Anu is the ancient Mesopotamian sky god and the patron god of Gilgamesh's home city of Uruk. However, this answer does not tell you: (1) what the meteorite has to do with Anu; (2) why the trapper Enkidu is compared to the meteorite of Anu; or (3) why Gilgamesh dreams that "the meteorite of Anu" falls on him (64, line 244). These are questions whose meaning require analysis, discussion, and interpretation in order to clarify. Indeed, it is likely that you may never reach a definitive answer to them, although the process of thinking critically about them will likely lead you to a number of insights about *The Epic of Gilgamesh*, its characters, and its themes. Think back to the flowchart for reading critically on the previous page: the phrase "meteorite of Anu" does not immediately make sense; its image is unexpected (why compare a man to a god's meteorite?); and it forms a pattern, as it is repeated several times during this part of the poem. Recognizing ambiguity means recognizing which questions are factual (who is Anu?) and which questions will open up into further reflection on the literature you are reading. In literature, the best questions are likely to be the ones you will never be able to answer fully, but that continue to prompt you to further discussion and investigation.

What Is World Literature?

All literature makes meaning by combining what is familiar with what is unfamiliar, and in this sense *all literature* has an element of world literature to it. As the twentieth-century Caribbean novelist

Jean Rhys put it, "Reading makes immigrants of us all. It takes us away from home, but more important, it finds homes for us everywhere." This experience is heightened in world literature, which the scholar and editor David Damrosch has defined as any literature that travels beyond its original moment of composition. World literature comes to us across one or more of the following gaps: across *time*, across *space*, across *cultures*, and across *languages*. One of the wonders of reading world literature is recognizing the common ground that exists across potentially great barriers, such as the eighth-century BCE epic, *The Iliad*, which is still considered one of the most realistic depictions of the experience of warfare ever composed. A second, perhaps greater, wonder is the way the differences of time, place, cultural context, and language transform our familiarity with this common ground into something completely new. However much we thought we knew about war before we read *The Iliad*, we will never look at it the same way again. When beginning to read a text of world literature, always be aware of the time, place, cultural context, and language from which it has come to you, and the ways in which its broader meanings have been formed by these factors. Whether or not you learn anything in depth about these elements in regard to a particular text, at the very least, read the introduction to the text you are assigned: it will provide the basics about time, place, culture, and language.

Time, Place, Cultural Context, and Language

We do not know when humans in communities first began telling stories and singing songs to one another, but we do know that the history of recorded literature dates back over 4,000 years to the earliest version of *The Epic of Gilgamesh*. Why do time and space matter? As the novelist I. P. Hartley put it in his twentieth-century novel *The Go-Between*, "The past is a foreign country. They do things differently there." Temporal distance raises practical constraints on reading: *The Epic of Gilgamesh* was lost from human memory for two thousand years before being rediscovered on a collection of thousands of clay tablet fragments excavated by a nineteenth-century Iraqi archaeologist. Very little of the writings of ancient Greece were available to medieval Europeans, who had few manuscripts and no knowledge of the language. Many ancient works survive only because of a single manuscript copied long after the original date of composition. Scholars of ancient literature are confronted with numerous gaps of meaning and ambiguities resulting from damage to the texts, errors made by copyists, and the difficulty of deciphering vanished languages. Many ancient texts were originally composed orally, meaning that they were performed for an audience rather than written, and each performance would be a different version of the same legend or story. The West African epic of Son-Jara or Sundiata, founder of the Mali Empire around 1250 CE, is still recited by performers today, who continue to rework the basic elements according to the world in which they now live (Damrosch, *How* 26).

The antiquity of many of the classics of world literature also means that they have been read by many different people and cultures over centuries and in different places, and that many different meanings have been attached to them. A fictionalized account of a Buddhist monk's legendary pilgrimage to India, the long sixteenth-century Chinese novel *Journey to the West* is an allegory of the individual's journey toward spiritual enlightenment. But it is also a rollicking adventure story, which is the way it was long received in English-speaking countries; an influential 1942 abridged translation focused exclusively on the fantastic adventures of Monkey, one of the major characters, while downplaying its religious context. Both elements are present in the original, and both contribute to the novel's meanings and our pleasure in reading it. Always try to be aware of your own expectations as a twenty-first-century reader. You will be able to recognize these expectations, in part, by your reaction to different components of a text. Like the translator Arthur Waley, you may respond more readily to the familiar narrative elements of Monkey's adventures than to the story's spiritual message. But perhaps that was part of the original novel's meaning as well: using an entertaining story to persuade its audience to think about the deeper values of its time, place, and culture. Awareness of the changing meanings of a text over time can also alert us to strategies that were intrinsic to the text to begin with.

Different cultures and, especially, different religions, form different expectations about literature itself. For example, for many contemporary readers, reading literature is primarily an aesthetic experience that touches on aspects of "real life," but also remains in many ways separate from it. Nevertheless, in many times, places, and cultures, as well as for innumerable individuals, literature is inseparable from the everyday life of the reader's (or listener's) community. This is especially the case of oral cultures and of religious literature. In oral cultures in Africa and elsewhere, the legal system of a community is expressed through the stories, sayings, songs, and other components of a tradition passed down through word of mouth. Many cultures hold the book of their religion to be literally true, a very different attitude than we would likely have toward a modern novel. Understanding the intended audience of a specific text can help us to situate the differences it demonstrates from our accustomed expectations of a work of fiction. This, in turn, allows us to make comparisons of similar themes between different cultures. Thus, Raymond-Jean Frontain writes about the different reaction students generally have to the epic heroes of Valmiki's *Ramayana* and Virgil's *Aeneid*: "Whereas [they] ultimately have little difficulty understanding Aeneas's sacrifice of personal desire for the good of an empire that will eventually glorify him as its founder, they are often confounded by Rama's commitment to honoring the word of his father, no matter what cost to the kingdom or himself" (344). Once we understand that different times, places, and cultures may have different assumptions about literature, we are in a position to make an informed comparison between texts.

Although texts themselves change over time, space, and cultures, we can trace themes across different works over time and space. This is one reason the academic field now known as world literature used to be called comparative literature. There are many potential grounds for comparison between two disparate texts. Some of the most common involve similarities in genre, in character and plot, in themes and imagery, and in parallel cultural patterns or social settings (Damrosch, *How* 47). As you work to make a comparison between two or more texts or elements of a task, always ask yourself about the principle of comparison you are using. If you cannot easily explain it, it is likely that your comparison needs to be thought out further.

Reading in Translation

The single greatest difference between reading world literature and English and American literature is language: most world literature was composed in a language other than English. You will probably be reading a translation. Indeed, given that there are thousands of languages spoken around the world today and many more that are no longer spoken, translation is a prerequisite for the very existence of world literature. Nevertheless, it is a mixed blessing. As the American poet Robert Frost once said, "Poetry is what is lost in translation." The act of translating is always a matter of choices, and it is never possible for a translation to capture all of the potential meanings of a text's original language. Most texts in world literature written in the fifteenth and sixteenth centuries are as challenging in their range vocabulary—and as archaic in their use of language—as Shakespeare's plays. You would never know this when reading a modern translation, however, since the English used by the translator is far closer to the English we readers are now accustomed to. When you do find a translator equal in stature to the original writer, as when Russian émigré novelist Vladimir Nabokov rendered Alexander Pushkin's classic narrative poem *Evgeny Onegin* into English, you will usually get a wholly new work of art, rather than a faithful translation. As poet Joseph Brodsky, a later twentieth-century Russian émigré put it, "Poetry is what is gained in translation." In certain cases, translations themselves can be influential. Since its first printing in 1611, the King James Version of the Bible has never been out of print, and remains the best-selling book of all time, its readers far outnumbering those of the original Hebrew, Aramaic, and Greek texts. Moreover, its distinctive style can be heard everywhere in English-language literature since the seventeenth century. Translation is a fact of life and, for the most part, a very welcome one.

What does it mean for you that you are reading most of the texts for this course in translation? Like other elements in world literature, such as time, space, and cultural context, translation is a factor in the way you understand what you read. Always remain aware of the fact that you are not reading the exact words written by the author of a text. Avoid overly weighting specific words, especially their sounds or connotations; always seek to ground any interpretation of a specific word or image in the broader sense of its context, or as part of a larger pattern within the text you are reading. Even if you do not read the original language of a text, you may find it instructive to compare a brief excerpt, especially if the text is a poem.

Be aware also of the presence of foreign words in the translations you read. Many works of literature themselves employ multiple languages in their vocabulary, and translators are faced with the choice of translating them. For instance, a number of nineteenth-century Russian novels contain extensive conversation in French, which was commonly used by the social elite. Many contemporary Latin American and Caribbean writers freely mix English and Spanish or French, posing something of a nightmare for translators, because when they translate the foreign language, the significance of English within it ceases to be felt. Similarly, the choice of English can itself be fraught with social significance. Nigerian writer Chinua Achebe defended his controversial choice to compose his novel *Things Fall Apart* (1958) and stories such as "Dead Men's Path" (discussed in Chapter 2) in English on several grounds. First, he observed, English, for better or worse, is the "national" language of Nigeria, the only language in which the many different ethnic groups can actually understand each other (Achebe, "African Writer" 852). Second, he wrote, English is a world language, providing world dissemination of his work, without the need for translation, "a new voice coming out of Africa, speaking of African experience in a world-wide language" (854). Finally, he concluded, "For me there is no other choice. I have been given this language and I am going to use it" (855). Many other writers would take the opposite stance, but for Achebe, at least, what was lost in translating his particular experience into a "world-wide language" was preferable to writing in his native language and then waiting for someone else to translate that experience into a more universal language.

There is no single right answer to this debate, but it is an important one to consider. As translator Lawrence Venuti observes, close attention to questions of translation is rewarding in itself, as it leads to a "renewed emphasis on reading closely and carefully" (95), which should always be the first step of reading any text, no matter the language.

2

KEEPING A RESPONSE JOURNAL

The specific details of a response journal will depend on your instructor, and may range from recording your immediate and personal reaction to what you have read, to notes, observations and questions, to preliminary analysis of specific passages of the text as the first step toward writing a formal paper. However, the form of the response journal is more standard. It is a relatively informal, low-stakes assignment. It will be fairly brief, no more than a few pages and sometimes less than one. It will be informal: that is, you will not usually be expected to include an introductory paragraph, a thesis, arguments, or a conclusion, or even to write an entire journal entry in paragraph form (you may choose to format parts of it as a list of elements in a pattern or as a series of questions). Nor will you normally be expected to follow a single line of thought from beginning to end. Your instructor will not necessarily collect them regularly; some will collect each entry as you complete it, others will collect them periodically, others may intend the journal solely as an aid to your preparation for class. Nevertheless, although this is an informal assignment, you should still observe the following conventions:

- Head each entry of your journal with your name, the name of the instructor, the name of the class, and the date in the upper left-hand corner. A title for each entry will either be optional or prohibited, but you may be asked to number the entries.
- Either type or handwrite each entry neatly. Some instructors prefer single-spaced entries, some double-spaced.

- Each sentence should be grammatical. Each word should be carefully chosen and correctly spelled.
- You should proofread *everything* you write before handing it in, and the journal is no exception.
- For your reference, and because you may be asked to resubmit all of the entries together at the end of the semester, keep them collected in one place, in a folder or binder.

An effective reading journal is an important component in the process of reading critically (see Chapter 1, p. 2), for it is the moment when you bring together all the different steps of reading and process them with a view toward the discussion and writing that are yet to come. Undertaken with enthusiasm and care, a reading journal pays back double the effort you put into it. Remember that some entries will be harder than others to write, and that some readings will engage you more readily than others. If you are having difficulty in responding to a reading, try talking about it with other students in the class, or emailing your instructor or attending office hours—often, talking over your reaction with others will help clarify your own thoughts. Your instructor is likely to provide some form of feedback on your journal entries. Make sure that you read any comments you receive and incorporate the suggestions into your work on future entries. If you are confused about any of the comments, be sure to visit your instructor during office hours.

Here is the entry of world literature student Amanda Wallace's reading journal on the short story "Dead Men's Path," by the Nigerian writer Chinua Achebe (b. 1930). Set in 1949, "Dead Men's Path" recounts the story of an ambitious and modern young man appointed to be headmaster in a rural school in Nigeria. He and his wife set out energetically to put the school into order. One day, they discover that the local villagers are allowed to continue to use an ancient path that runs right through the school compound and garden. The path connects the village shrine with its burial site. When the headmaster fences off the compound, the village priest comes to complain. The headmaster dismisses the concern as superstition and refuses to take down the fence. When a woman dies in childbirth soon after, the villagers assume it is due to the blocked path. Influenced by a diviner, they tear up the fence and hedges and all of the flowerbeds, and also pull down a school building. On a visit of inspection, the "white Supervisor" concludes that a tribal war is developing.

You can follow Amanda's further work with this story in subsequent chapters.

Wallace 1

Amanda Wallace
Professor Pike
Introduction to World Literature
12 March 2011

Reading Journal Entry 5

I knew from the title that the story would be something about a dead person, but I didn't know what. I also wasn't sure why there were lots of them ("dead men"). But it feels like something was haunted. While I was reading it, I wasn't sure who I was supposed to like. I felt sorry for Michael Obi but not so much for his wife, who was competitive and petty, except when her garden was ruined. The village priest was old and he didn't really make much of a case. When he said, "Let the hawk perch and let the eagle perch" (45) I think he meant live and let live. But then he didn't when they trampled the garden. The white Supervisor made me wonder about the headmaster, but then I wasn't sure if I should believe his view of things either. So the first question I want to ask is: who is right in the story and who is wrong?

Notice things that surprised you and then follow up by looking at examples, as the characters listed here.

Try to follow a connected list of observations with a question.

I noticed two main patterns: the path and the garden and young and old / old and new. The path is in the title, but the garden is the setting everybody is fighting in. First, the garden is "beautiful" and "modern and delightful" (44) then the old woman is caught crossing it. Then Obi puts up a fence with barbed wire and then the village priest comes to see him. He calls it an "ancestral pathway" (45) and the headmaster calls it a "highway" (45)—that's a big difference. There are two solutions. The headmaster wants a detour in the path and the vil-

Look for patterns and then list the elements that make up the patterns.

lagers want it to go through. The break in the pattern comes when they tear up the garden and the Supervisor sees a "tribal war situation" (46). What's the relation between the path and the garden and what makes it so important to everybody?

Look for where the pattern breaks.

Old and new: the word "young" is repeated four times in the first page, referring to Obi and his wife. The word "old" and "older" is also repeated. It refers to "less educated" headmasters (44) and to the old woman using the path and the village priest. This pattern doesn't really break, except that near the end the woman who dies having a child is referred to as "young" (46). She's one of the villagers, but maybe she had modern views? Or is there some other reason she is called young? The school seems connected to the "new" since it is Obi's school and it has a new garden. The path is called "almost disused" (45), which makes it sound old. Does the fight between old and new have to happen?

More questions:

- Is the headmaster white or black? Why doesn't the narrator tell us?
- Why make the wife so unsympathetic?
- Why does the Supervisor call it a "tribal war"?
- Why is it called "Dead Men's Path" when it's mostly about the headmaster?
- Are we supposed to believe that the dead men travel on the path and the other beliefs?

3

PARTICIPATING IN CLASS DISCUSSION

Most world literature courses you take will have a participation component included within the final grade. If your class is discussion-based, this probably means regular participation in class discussion; if it is lecture-based, it means asking questions of the professor and/or participating in discussion sections distinct from the main lecture course. Not all students are immediately comfortable speaking up in class, and your instructor will be aware of this. If you are having trouble speaking up in class, the first thing to do is to talk to your instructor. This will show that you are concerned about your participation and the instructor will be able to help you with strategies for participating more fully. Even if you are not contributing regularly, your body language and behavior in class can give important signals that you are following the discussion and thinking about it. Arrive on time to class, and don't get up in the middle—stay put until class is truly over. Always bring your book to class, along with paper and a writing utensil or a laptop (if permitted) for notes. Always turn off your cell phone, pager, and other electronic devices for the duration of class. Sit up straight and make eye contact with your instructor and fellow students when they are talking. If you find yourself getting restless or sleepy in class, remember the cardinal rule: the more you talk, the more awake you will be, the more interested you will be, and the faster the class will go.

What do I say? If you are keeping a reading journal, use your journal entries to generate material for classroom discussion. If you are having trouble coming up with ideas for questions, try talking about your class readings before class with other students in the class. You can even plan questions or topics to bring up together. If you are still getting used to participating, ask a simple question, ideally near the beginning of class. Amanda Wallace's journal entry in Chapter 2 contains a number of such questions: for instance, "Is the headmaster white or black?" and "Why does the Supervisor call it a 'tribal war'?" These are good questions because they will lead to further discussion, rather than a simple yes or no answer. You also have the option of asking informational questions (just make sure they are not already answered in the introduction to your reading or in other class materials): "What was happening in Nigeria in 1949 that provides a background for these events?" or "What were the traditional religious beliefs of the people in the village?" Or, you can ask specific questions about the language of the text (this story was originally written in English). "Why does Obi look older than he is to his wife?" or "What does the village elder mean when he says 'I have no more words to say'?" When you ask questions, always try to frame them, as in the examples here, in an open-ended way rather than in a way that forecloses more discussion, and generally avoid making value judgments on the reading or the characters in the reading. Try to formulate questions in terms of the author's choices rather than in absolute terms: "Why make the wife so unsympathetic?" versus "Why is the wife so unsympathetic?"

You can also ask more ambitious questions or make observations that incorporate your own analysis, as Amanda could do, based on her reading journal: "I noticed a pattern of conflict between the school garden and the path. The wife's garden covers up the path and then the villagers destroy the garden. It seems as if there is no way they can both exist together." "The words 'young' and 'old' are used a lot in the story. 'Young' almost always refers to the headmaster and his wife and 'old' to the path, the old woman, and the village priest. But there's one exception. Is it important that the woman who dies is young?" Remember, whether your question is simple or complicated, your instructor will be delighted that you are participating, not only for what you have to add to discussion, but because the more students that participate, the more engaging the class is for everyone. Once you are comfortable in the class, consider also responding directly to other students' comments and questions.

4

PREPARING AND GIVING A CLASS PRESENTATION

A class presentation can take several forms. Some instructors simply assign certain students each class day to come especially prepared with questions and topics for discussion. For this sort of presentation, simply adapt material according to the instructions for preparation of journal entries and class discussion in Chapters 2 and 3. The most common sort of presentation is one that provides historical, cultural, or critical context for the primary reading assigned for class. Your instructor may assign you a particular source or set of sources, usually either books or articles. These will usually be in a class packet, on library reserves, or in some other easily accessible form. Or, your instructor may require that you research and choose your own sources (for more on finding sources, see Chapter 6). Make sure that your sources adequately meet your instructor's requirements, particular in terms of number of sources, currency (avoid sources older than 1990), and scholarly rigor (unless otherwise instructed, choose sources only from scholarly presses and refereed journals). Use Web pages and other Internet sources only if explicitly instructed to do so. When in doubt, always check with the instructor. As with all assignments, begin sufficiently in advance that if anything goes wrong, or you have questions, you have time to ask your instructor for assistance. This is especially the case if you are giving a multimedia or PowerPoint presentation.

Here are some tips applicable to just about any kind of academic (or professional) presentation:

- Stick to your topic. Avoid clever asides and digressions, no matter how entertaining you think they might be.
- If you are working with a group, make sure you meet early, divide the labor, and make clear the expectation that all members of the group will carry an equal load. If you are having problems motivating any members of the group, ask your instructor for advice or help.
- Make a works-cited list. Have it at the end of your printed presentation in case you are asked about it, and as the last slide of a PowerPoint presentation.
- Avoid using images for decoration or effect. Only use them if they are part of the substance of your presentation.
- Make sure you know and stick to your time limit. This means you will have to rehearse and time your presentation. A good rule of thumb for a typed-out presentation is two minutes per double-spaced page; so, about two and a half pages for a five-minute presentation and four to five pages for ten minutes.
- If you are presenting as part of a group, make sure that you are clear about different roles during the presentation. It is usually important that all members of a group speak for at least part of the time.
- Make sure that you know how to correctly pronounce all proper names and technical terms in your presentation.
- Always practice your presentation ahead of time, preferably out loud and in front of an audience, until you are comfortable giving it and don't trip over any part of it.
- Never practice your presentation to the point that you have every part of it memorized. You will sound like an automaton.
- If using technology, assume that something will go wrong and have a backup plan, such as a printed copy of your Power-Point slides. Arrive early to have time to set up.
- While presenting, always look up as often as you can to make eye contact with your audience. If you are nervous making eye contact, choose a particular spot or spots among the audience, or just behind them, and look there instead.
- If you read your presentation, make sure you rehearse a few moments of "ad-libbed" lines, even if you memorize them. That will help to vary the rhythm of your reading.

- Don't talk too quickly. If you have too much material, cut some of it. If you can't help yourself, stop to take a drink of water, straighten your collar, or fix your hair.
- Don't talk too slowly. You'll put everybody to sleep no matter how interesting your presentation is.
- Be ready for questions afterwards. That's the most rewarding part of the whole thing.

The print form of a researched presentation follows a similar format to the research paper discussed in Chapter 7. There will likely be less focus on a developed thesis and sustained argument. Nevertheless, you should think in similar terms: a clear and organized presentation of research focused on explaining a particular facet or general background of a literary work you have read in your class. A five-minute presentation on the Igbo and Christian missionary context of "Dead Men's Path" could easily have been drawn from the research that went into Amanda's paper in Chapter 7. To provide an example of a PowerPoint presentation entitled "Christian Missionaries in Igboland," we have designed a sample slide based on the same research:

Some Pieces of Igbo/Christian History in "Dead Men's Path"

- The first Christian mission in Igboland was in Onitsha (Isichei 211).
- Obi's modern methods lead him to argue that the "old and superannuated teachers ...would be better employed as traders in the Onitsha market" (Achebe 44).
  - **Does the history of Onitsha influence this reference?**

- The Igbo attitude toward religion: "The Igbo response which is most often given in mission records was to state that all religions worship the same God, and that the particular forms they take are those appropriate to the needs and forms of each society – so that Igbo religion was appropriate for Igboland, and Christianity was suitable for both black and white Europeans." (Isicheit 214).
- The village priest's advice to "Let the hawk perch and let the eagle perch" (Achebe 45).
  - **Does this proverb reflect Igbo attitudes toward religious openness as described by Isichei?**

- Early success of the Onitsha boys and girls schools established by the late 19th century by missionaries. The Igbo came primarily because of interest in learning English and math, while conversion was the main goal of the missionaries (Bastian 146–47).
- Presence of Ndume Central School in "Dead Men's Path"
  - **Why is the Christian religion never directly discussed even though if Obi is sent by "the Mission authorities" (Achebe 44) he must be Christian?**

5

WRITING A
LITERARY ANALYSIS AND
OTHER TYPES OF PAPERS

In this chapter we discuss the process of writing a literary analysis as well as other common types of papers you will be asked to write in a world literature class. The literary analysis is the backbone of academic writing on literature. Although different instructors will vary the length, the basic structure of the literary analysis paper is as follows:

- Student name, instructor name, course title, and date in the upper left-hand corner, double-spaced.
- Pages should be numbered consecutively, with last name followed by page number, in the upper right-hand corner.
- Title of the paper, centered on the page, capitalized except for internal prepositions.
- Introductory paragraph, including your thesis statement.
- Body paragraphs, with each paragraph introducing and providing evidence to support a different facet of your argument.
- Concluding paragraph, restating your thesis and suggesting further possibilities, such as loose ends that your argument couldn't account for, conclusions derived from your thesis, or suggestions for further directions in which your arguments might lead.
- Works-cited list at the end, always on a new page. In a literary analysis, this list typically includes the primary text you are analyzing, unless your instructor has explicitly directed you to use secondary sources in your paper.

Generating a Thesis from Your Reading Notes or Reading Journal

Begin work on your paper by rereading the text and reviewing your notes and any prior writing you have done on the text. Make a list of relevant passages from the text that you may use in the paper. Then start writing out the arguments your notes lead you to. For some students, this process works best as notes and outline. Other students, including Amanda Wallace, prefer to work visually. After reviewing her work on "Dead Men's Path," Amanda decided to return to her question of the title as a way of organizing her thoughts on the patterns of path/garden and old/new. Here is the idea map she drew up in the process of brainstorming, along with some of our notes on her work:

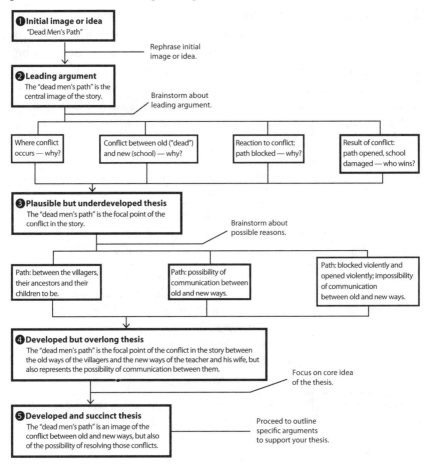

Some writers find it easier to develop ideas through writing than through planning, and find it difficult to devise a thesis before they start writing. Nevertheless, if this describes you as a writer, it is still preferable to begin with a makeshift thesis, even if you are dissatisfied with it, as it will help you organize the shape of your first draft and leave you less to revise later. Be sure to leave time for at least two revisions. You will probably find your thesis at the end of your initial draft. Your second draft will then function as the standard first draft, and you will require a third draft, since no paper should be submitted without at least one thorough revision.

Types of Papers and Their Theses

The most common evaluated writing assignment in world literature courses is the literary analysis paper, but there are other types of papers you may also be asked to write. Here are some of the other types of papers common in a world literature course, along with a sample thesis, where applicable:

Type of Paper	*Definition (with thesis in italics)*
Response	An initial reaction, including observations and questions.
Explication	A line-by-line analysis.
Textual analysis (or thesis-driven explication)	*The "dead men's path" is an image of the conflict between old and new ways, but also of the possibility of resolving those conflicts.*
Comparison (also known as Compare & Contrast)	An analysis of similarities and differences between two or more texts. *The titles in Chinua Achebe's "Dead Men's Path" and Sherman Alexie's "This Is What It Means to Say Phoenix, Arizona" present images of the conflict between different ways of life, but also of the possibility of resolving those conflicts, although in different ways.*
Argumentative	A paper that takes a strong position on issues brought out by its thesis. *"Dead Men's Path" presents an image of the conflict between old and new ways that can be resolved only through violence.*

Research	A paper that combines textual analysis with fact-based research (see Chapter 7). *"Dead Men's Path" presents an image of the conflict between old and new ways that occurred all over Africa in the years after World War II.*

The Comparison Paper

Before we continue with Amanda's literary analysis paper, here is a guide to a common variant on the literary analysis, the comparison paper, which is basically two literary analyses put together. Often, when making a comparison, you will notice elements about each text that you had not seen in isolation, and a comparison can even be a useful exercise in preparation for the analysis of a single text. All comparisons begin with a framework of similarity and then look for differences within that framework. It is the interaction of similarity and difference that creates meaning in a comparison. The best way to begin making a comparison is by making lists. You can write your list as an idea map or in simple columns. The table below suggests some possible questions to ask and categories to use for generating lists to begin developing a comparison paper.

WRITER'S **GUIDE**

Making Comparisons

Comparing Formal Qualities

- *Genre:* Are the texts poems, short stories, plays, or essays? Within each genre, are they a particular type (e.g., argumentative essay, explication, comparison)? Do the texts meet or not meet expectations about their genre?

- *Title:* What is the relation between the title and the text? Are titles of different texts similar or different?

- *Speaker/narrator:* Who is the speaker of the poem or the narrator of the story? Is there a first-person speaker (I) or a third person (he, she)? What information does the speaker present directly to us and what do we have to interpret?

- *Point of view:* Is the point of view limited to a single character, to several characters? Is it omniscient (unlimited)?

- *Time frame:* Is the text narrated as if it were happening as you are reading it, or in retrospect, looking back into the past? How much time passes?

- *Type of action:* Are the events described an isolated sequence occurring once, or a habitual activity?

- *Structure:* Parse poems; segment stories or essays. Are poems broken into stanzas? Do they rhyme? Are stories or essays divided into parts? Do plays have similar act and scene divisions?
- *Mood:* What is the mood (happy, melancholy, solitary, satisfied, dissatisfied, bored) of the text?
- *Language and imagery:* Do the texts use figurative language? Striking images?

Comparing Descriptive and Narrative Qualities
- *Setting:* What are the similarities and differences in setting?
- *Description:* What people, places, and things are described, and in what way?
- *Characterization:* Who are the characters? What are they like, how are they described?
- *Plot:* What events occur? What actions do the characters perform? Which characters do what?

Looking for Patterns, Themes, and Arguments
- Are there any repeating words, images or themes? Do they form any particular patterns? Are there any breaks in the pattern?
- What relationship does each text establish with the outside world? Do they connect to broad social themes (like the conflict between old and new ways identified by Amanda Wallace in "Dead Men's Path")?

From List to Thesis
- Summarize your findings as a list of patterns, or connections between, the similarities and differences in the texts you are comparing. Be selective: choose what seem to you to be the most significant rather than the most obvious patterns and topics.
- Analyze your list of patterns, looking for connections between them. Look for connections within each text, and connections between texts.
- Work with these connections to formulate an argument and thesis about what the texts share and what makes them different.
- Use your list of patterns to outline your argument paragraph by paragraph. There are two ways to structure the body of a comparison paper: you can discuss the texts one after the other, or you can discuss them together according to each aspect of your argument.

Outlining the Parts of the Paper

Once you have determined the thesis of your paper, you are ready to draw up an outline of the paper and the specific arguments you will use. This guide draws examples from Amanda Wallace's literary analysis paper reproduced at the end of this chapter:

1. **Title.** Often the best title will come to you once you finish your initial draft, but make sure you have a working title from the

beginning so that you don't forget to add it later on. *Amanda's working title: "The Image of the Dead Men's Path."*

2. **Introductory paragraph.** This paragraph should provide basic information about the text (or texts, if you are doing a comparison paper) you are writing about, summarize the different parts of your paper, and, of course, state your thesis. You should not quote from the text, summarize the plot, or provide close reading in your introductory paragraph.

   Amanda's thesis: "The dead men's path is an image of the conflict between old and new ways, but also of the possibility of resolving those conflicts."

3. **Body paragraphs.** The body of a two- to three-page paper will have two to four paragraphs; a five-page paper will have four to eight.

   a. *The dead men's path is the path between the villagers, their ancestors, and their children-to-be.*

   b. *The path blocked violently and opened violently; impossibility of communication between old and new ways.*

   c. *The dead men's path as the possibility of communication between old and new ways.*

4. **Concluding paragraph.** Often, this will be the place to bring in related material that you were not otherwise able to fit into your argument.

   Amanda's conclusion: "The image of the garden suggests there is also a possibility of communication through the new ways."

Putting the Words on the Page

You cannot start revising unless you have something to revise, so start writing! Use your outline to help build the paper, sentence by sentence, and paragraph by paragraph. Try to find a place to write where you are not likely to be interrupted and will not be easily distracted. Turn off all electronic devices except your computer, and disable your Internet connection (or turn off your computer and write the first draft by hand). The more you can concentrate on writing, the more cohesive your first draft will be, and the fewer revisions you will need to do later. Use a paper-writing checklist like the one that follows here to avoid making common mistakes.

We have included Amanda's second draft of a two- to three-page literary analysis here, along with some general comments on the form of the paper.

WRITER'S **GUIDE**

Tips for Avoiding Common Paper-Writing Errors

A. Spelling and Word Choice

• Avoid the following common mistakes:

affect/effect: The light affects his eyes; they effected a clever settlement.

accept/except: He could not accept the consequences; except for us

two/too/to: two heads; too far; to the limit

rite/right: rite of passage; right turn; bill of rights

there/their/they're: There is only one explanation for their behavior: they're crazy.

where/were: Where were you?

loose/lose: loose-fitting; nothing to lose

lead/led: She leads now where once you led.

whose/who's: Whose fault is it? Who's there?

its/it's: It's not too late to save its life.

• *Prepositions:* Are you using the right ones?

• *Proper capitalization:* Capitalize at the beginning of a sentence and the beginning of a quotation. Check your dictionary for words, such as adjectives of nationality, that are always capitalized.

• *Names:* Refer to the *speaker* in a poem and the *narrator* in a story rather than using the author's name. Refer to characters in a film or television show by their proper names (not the actors'): you can find this information at imdb.com.

B. Syntax

• *Sentence fragments:* Does each of your sentences have a subject and a verb?

• *Run-on sentences:* Can you parse your sentences? Do all of the parts fit together grammatically?

• *Subject/verb agreement:* Is the subject singular or plural? "*One* of them *is* right but the *others are* wrong"

C. Diction

• *Punctuation:* Are your commas, semicolons, colons, and full stops necessary and in the right place? Remember, a colon introduces a list, and only a semicolon can join two independent clauses without a conjunction: "It was raining; I ran." "It was raining, but I ran." "It was a mess: hail, freezing rain, and sleet."

• *Word order:* Are the words in an order that actually says what you want to say?

• *Tenses:* Is the base tense for your critical writing in the present tense, not the past? "In this poem, a woman *is* eating blackberries."

- *Dangling modifiers:* Are your modifiers in the right place? Avoid sentences like this: "Running from the scene of the crime, the police arrested the suspect."

- *Awkward phrasing:* Have you written a sentence that may be grammatical, but that no one will be able to follow?

D. Structure

- *Thesis/topic sentence:* Is there one in the first paragraph? Do you know what your argument is?

- *Paragraphing:* Does each paragraph contain a topic sentence and argument?

- *Citations:* Do you analyze each passage you cite? Do you have at least one line of discussion for every line cited?

E. Style

- *Thesis and argument:* Is your thesis clear, engaging, and arguable? Do the arguments in the body of your paper relate to the claim your thesis makes? Do you produce concrete evidence to support your arguments?

- *Demonstration/critique/analysis versus assertion/opinion/evaluation:* Does your paper *show* how your thesis works through specific examples, comparisons, and detailed analysis, or does it merely *state* its conclusions as if they were self-evident?

- *Inconclusive/glosses over/closes down versus draws conclusions/interprets/raises questions:* Does your paper explore different approaches and/or aspects of a related set of issues (good), or does it reductively argue a single yes-or-no issue all the way (not good)?

- *Is your argument dictating your paper structure* or *are you just summarizing the plot?* If you are recounting events in the same order as the text you are writing about presents them, then you are not making an argument.

- *Adjectives (concrete versus abstract):* Do your adjectives impart useful information that helps visualize or imagine the nouns they modify (*tall, yellow, detailed*), or do they reflect value judgments and/or undefinable qualities (*great, bad, beautiful, ugly*)?

F. Apparatus

- *Text titles:* Have you italicized or underlined book and film titles? Titles of short texts (like poems and short stories) should be in quotation marks.

- *Citation:* Have you cited short excerpts (four lines or less) within the flow of text, double-spaced, and using quotation marks? Have you cited longer excerpts (more than four lines) separately: indented, double-spaced, and without quotation marks? (See Appendix A for further details on citation.)

- *Referencing and documentation:* Have you provided page references and bibliographical information for any source you have cited? Have you properly documented any idea, phrasing, or passage that you borrowed from another source? (See Appendix A for further details on documentation.)

- *Formatting:* Are you using a 12-point font and 1-inch margins? Are you following the length and formatting guidelines given in the assignment prompt? Is your paper as a whole doing what the assignment prompt asks you to do?

G. Process

- Have you rewritten your first draft at least once? Have you run the spell-check *and* proofread your writing?
- In a state of doubt or confusion?
  - Check a paper-writing handbook such as the *MLA Handbook for Research Papers.*
  - Ask a friend or classmate to read and comment on what you have so far.
  - Consult the helpful folk at your school's writing center.
  - Talk to your teacher during office hours.

Wallace 1

Amanda Wallace
Professor Pike
Introduction to World Literature
26 February 2011

Where Does the Dead Men's Path Lead?

The title of Chinua Achebe's short story "Dead Men's Path" introduces the main image of the story, but it does not explain what it means. It seems more of a mystery: who are the dead men? The story eventually suggests three possible roles for the path. In the traditional Igbo belief, it provides a route for the ancestors of the villagers to visit and for children to come to the village to be born. In the conflict that arises with the young headmaster, the path is the source of violence and destruction. And in its image as a path uniting past and future, it suggests the possibility of dialogue between old and new. The dead men's path is an image of the conflict between old and new ways, but also of the possibility of resolving those conflicts.

Despite its presence in the title, the dead men's path does not appear until the middle of the story, where it stands for the traditions of the village. However, looking back, it may be present in the references to "old teachers" in the first part of the story. The main focus of the first part is on the new ways brought to the village by the

Refined from the working title (p. 23), the new title is more specific, and alludes to the thesis in its question.

The opening paragraph is the place to outline the parts of your paper.

A usual location for the thesis is at the conclusion of the first paragraph.

Try to organize each paragraph in relation to your overall thesis.

Wallace 2

"young headmaster" and his "young wife" (44), and the "dream gardens" planted by Nancy in the school compound (45). Although apparently they had never noticed the path, "an old woman from the village" (45) hobbling across it brings it to their attention. In his response, the headmaster connects the path to "pagan ritual" (45), which he views as incompatible with the goals of his school. He signals this view by planting "heavy sticks" and "barbed wire" at the places where the path enters and leaves the school compound (45). When the second, "old" figure appears, he refers to Obi as "son" and explains to him that the "whole life of the village depends" on the path, because "[o]ur dead relatives visit us by it. But most important, it is the path of children coming in to be born" (45). The violent response of the villagers to the blocking of the path suggests how strongly they believe in the importance of the path as a link between their past and their future.

    The aggressive action of the headmaster in fencing the path with barbed wire and the more aggressive response of the villagers suggests that there is no possibility that the old ways can communicate with the new ways. This impossibility of communication is demonstrated by the two proverb-like pronouncements of the village priest. First, he suggests a compromise, accepting Obi's "duty . . . to teach your children to laugh at such ideas," and trying to avoid a quarrel: "What I always say is: let the hawk perch and let the eagle perch" (45). Live and let live: the birds may be different, but they are both powerful predators and perhaps they can coexist. The suggestion by the "young headmaster" that the villagers make a detour, including a joke about the ancestors, makes it clear that he does not understand the old man's argument. The "old priest" seems to conclude the same thing, responding that, "I have no more words to say" (46). Words have proven useless and the only thing that appears to work is action. But rather than tell us the con-

In-text citation referring to the works-cited list. There is only one work cited, so only the page number is needed in parentheses following the quote. (For more on in-text citation, see Appendix A.)

When incorporating quoted text into your own sentence, be sure that the syntax of the quoted material agrees with your own language.

Use the topic sentence of each paragraph to establish a transition from the previous paragraph and to introduce its main idea.

Wallace 3

sequences of the villagers' destructive response to the death of the young woman, Achebe concludes with a strange quote from the report of the visiting "white Supervisor," which criticizes the "misguided zeal" of the "new headmaster" (46). In conclusion, Michael Obi appears to have misunderstood the desires of his superiors, the villagers have been unable to understand Michael Obi, and the Supervisor, fearing a "tribal war situation," seems to have misunderstood what has happened, too. Without the path, there is no possibility of any kind of understanding.

The final sentence of a paragraph should sum up its argument.

But the story may not be quite as hopeless as it appears. In applying the image of the path as the possibility of communication between old and new ways to the story as a whole, it is possible to see the school as somehow resembling the path. After all, it links the old teachers, the ones who understand the role of the path and continue to let the villagers use it, with the new one, who is always looking toward the future. Perhaps this is the reason that the one time the adjective "young" is not applied to Michael Obi or his wife, it refers to the "young woman" who dies in childbirth (46). It is not said if the baby survives. Because it passes directly through the school, the path suggests that the school itself has some kind of role to play in the life of the village. In order for the old ways to somehow coexist with the new, the path must be allowed somehow to continue to pass through the school. Otherwise the old and the new will be severed, and there will be destruction in the village.

Often in literature, there is more than one way of looking at the same images and events.

In this way, the dead men's path in this story makes an image of the conflict between old and new ways, but also suggests it could be possible to resolve those conflicts. The difficulty of resolving seems to have something to do with the garden. It is because of the garden that Mike and Nancy notice the path and to protect the garden from figures such as the "old woman" walking "through

The concluding paragraph should restate the thesis.

In the concluding paragraph, also try to introduce

Wallace 4

a marigold flowerbed" (45) that the fence is built. And it is the garden that suffers the full force of the anger of the villagers. Like the path, the garden is an image of nature, "a place of beauty" and life (45) but carefully tended and needing protection. Almost invisible, the dead man's path is like a ghost haunting the school. But it is also a ghost that helps to lead children into the world, just as the school, in a way, also does. It is as if Achebe sees both ways as necessary, but cannot yet see how they can perch together in the same space, like the hawk and the eagle.

something new to your argument, often something that didn't fit the main thesis but is closely related to it, or opens it up in a new direction.

Wallace 5

Work Cited

Achebe, Chinua. "Dead Men's Path." *Literature: A World of Writing*. Ed. David L. Pike and Ana M. Acosta. New York: Pearson Longman, 2011. 44–46. Print.

Include all works cited in the paper on a new page following MLA format (see Appendix A).

6

Conducting Research and Compiling an Annotated Bibliography

Perhaps more than any other form of writing you will do, the research paper is a step-by-step process—and you will have learned most if not all of the steps already. To write a research paper, you just have to put those steps together. Follow each step carefully and thoroughly, and your paper will take shape before your eyes.

Finding a Topic

The first step in writing a research paper is finding and limiting yourself to a specific and clearly defined paper topic. Make sure that you reserve plenty of time to think about your topic, and do some preliminary research, either in the library or on the Internet, in order to make sure that the subject actually interests you and that there are enough acceptable sources available. An ideal topic will usually be something unusual enough that not too much has been written about it, but not so unusual that you are unable to find any scholarly sources to use. Finding the perfect topic is the matter of matching your interests to the constraints of the research paper form, the instructor's requirements, and your course's particular focus.

Once you have chosen a topic, you will then need to refine it to the point that it is acceptable both to yourself and to your instructor. You will usually be asked to submit your topic as a written paragraph. Like a summary of the paper to come, your topic will reflect your initial, broad reading, and will help you decide the specific direction to take once you begin research in earnest and start working on your annotated bibliography. Also like a summary, it will not yet have an argument or a thesis, but if done right will help in synthesizing your initial thoughts in the direction of an argument. Many first-time writers of research papers are tempted by what seems the safe route of a purely historical topic—a biography of a writer, a study of a specific place or event. A college-level research paper is argument-based, however, and it is difficult to conceive a good thesis and sustain an original and cohesive argument if you are merely cutting and pasting other people's research on a topic.

The assignment for Amanda Wallace's class required that she use a previous paper as the basis for the research paper. When she decided to use her literary analysis of "Dead Men's Path" (Chapter 5, p. 26) as the basis for a research paper on Christian missionaries in Igboland, she wanted to investigate how her interpretation of conflict in the story was related to actual events that may have provided a historical context for the story. Preliminary readings in a biography of Achebe and sources on the history of Christianity in Achebe's native country of Nigeria helped her think about the direction she wanted her research to take in a paper topic:

Wallace 1

Amanda Wallace
Professor Pike
Introduction to World Literature
2 March 2011

Paper Topic

Chinua Achebe's "Dead Men's Path" is set during the period after Christian missionaries had come to Igboland, part of Nigeria. This happened in the late 19th century. The first modern schools were run by missionaries, including one in Onitsha, mentioned in the story. Igbo people wanted to learn English and to read and write, but didn't always want to become Christians. The story is set in 1949, which is much later, but Nigeria was still a colony of Britain and there is still a conflict between old and new. In this paper, I will discuss how the missionaries

Before you start your in-depth research, you will need some basic facts about your subject.

Always have an idea about the broad topic of your paper, even if you are not sure

Wallace 2

came to Igboland and how they conflicted with Igbo beliefs. My sources will include sources on Achebe's life and on this theme in his writing. I will also research sources on Christian missionaries in Nigeria.

about the thesis or the details yet.

A paper topic should list the categories of sources you will be researching, even if you are not required to list specific sources yet.

Finding and Evaluating Your Sources

Perhaps the most important step in writing a successful research paper is choosing the correct sources. Good sources will inspire you, push you in directions you hadn't yet thought of, and provide you with the essential information you need to formulate a strong thesis and carry through a solid argument. If a source fulfills none of these needs, it will not be of much help to you in writing your paper. Your initial probing into a topic may or may not have led you directly to the sources you will need for your paper; in either case, once you start assembling the material that will actually go into your paper, you need to do so with great care and careful organization. Proper documentation and note taking at this stage will streamline the writing process and save you a lot of work later on, both for the paper itself and for the **annotated bibliography**, or summary and evaluation of your sources that you will likely be required to write beforehand. Remember, if you have any questions about any stage in this process, ask a librarian or your instructor. Always ask *sooner* rather than *later*.

Primary Sources and Secondary Sources

Most research papers will include both **primary sources**—texts and documents from the time period of your topic or written by your subject—and **secondary sources**—history and criticism written in the present day about your subject. It may be that your only primary source is the world literature text(s) you read, which provided the initial idea for your paper topic, as in the case of Amanda's primary source, "Dead Men's Path."

Although it is tempting in today's multimedia world to include illustrations in your paper for aesthetic appeal, the only place you should include an illustration for its own sake is (if authorized by your instructor) on the title page. Avoid including an image just because it is "cool" or to show what someone or something looked like. Instead, use the text of your paper to make clear descriptions, unless you plan to analyze an image as part of your argument.

Working in the Library and on the Internet

Your first resort for both primary and secondary sources will be your school library. You can begin this research from wherever you have access to the library's online catalog. Searching a catalog is a skill worth refining. For Amanda's research, she had the option of searching by *author* for writings by Chinua Achebe and *subject* ("Nigeria—church history" or "Nigeria—colonization"). Books will provide a good introduction to your topic; they may also turn out to be either too broad or too detailed for your needs. Most research papers use a combination of books and scholarly articles or essays. The best way to find the articles you need, if you are researching a literary topic, is the *MLA International Bibliography*, a compendium of references to scholarly writing on literature published annually by the Modern Language Association (MLA) and available on CD-ROM, in print versions, and online from most libraries. The *MLA International Bibliography* indexes books, articles, and book chapters and can be searched by author, title of work, subject, keyword, or a combination of the four. Library resources also include various databases and print guides for research on nonliterary topics, or for primary research in newspapers and nonacademic serial publications (magazines). The *Reader's Guide to Periodical Literature* is available in both print and CD-ROM versions, as are indexes to many different newspapers, as well as specialized indexes for specific subjects.

You may also choose to use an Internet search engine to look for sources. You may find such a search useful in the early stages of your research to get a handle on your topic. But remember that there are very few topics on which no scholarly criticism has been written, and that these should be your main sources. Many instructors will limit the number of purely Internet sources they allow, or will not allow them at all. Make sure that you are aware of these guidelines before you begin your research.

Evaluating and Organizing Your Sources

As you begin assembling sources, and as the first sources you read point you toward further sources, you will find it helpful to compile a **working bibliography**, an evolving list of sources you have found, sources you have read, and sources that you will need. As you read, you can add notes, summaries, paraphrases, and quotations you may use in your final paper. From your working bibliography, you will compose your **annotated bibliography** and the **works-cited list** for your research paper. Before including any source in your working bibliography, assess its suitability for inclusion in a research paper. The first level of assessment is whether or not the source is suitably rigorous and scholarly. Regardless of whether you conduct your search on-site or online, you will encounter a wide variety of sources. We can categorize them as follows, in descending order of suitability for a research paper:

1. *Academic journals and monographs.* Because they are peer-reviewed by experts in the subject, academic journals (collections of articles) and monographs (book-length studies) are held to a more rigorous set of standards than other sources. You will find that specialists have written scholarly articles and monographs on your topic, their arguments will be original, and their sources will be fully documented. Most, if not all, of the sources for a research paper should be drawn from academic journals and monographs unless otherwise authorized by your instructor. Your library's online portal will include a number of databases containing academic journals; your library may also provide access to online versions of certain academic monographs. Nearly all academic journals devoted to the study of literature are indexed by the MLA, which can likely be accessed through your library; some reliable and commonly available article databases are Project Muse, JSTOR, ProQuest Research Library, and Academic Search Premier (EBSCO).

2. *General histories, surveys, and biographies.* Usually written for a nonspecialized audience by specialized scholars, these sources will reliably situate a topic within a broad context. Useful for background research, they are unlikely to give you the kind of detail and complexity you will need to develop a good thesis.

3. *Newspapers and other general periodicals.* Accessed either in print form, online, or through databases, newspapers of record such as the *New York Times* or the *Washington Post* are acceptable secondary sources, especially for current events or contemporary writers; other newspapers and popular periodicals are generally acceptable only as primary sources—for example, an essay by Achebe first published in newspaper form.

4. *Encyclopedia articles, general reference works, and university-based Web pages.* Peer-reviewed and held to an external set of standards, these sources can provide basic information and point you toward more in-depth sources. Due to their brevity and to their broad focus, however, they are not suitable as sources for a college paper except for brief biographical or factual information, such as the date of colonization of Nigeria or a list of the writings of Chinua Achebe.

5. *Opinion-based sources: blogs, personal Web pages, op-ed pieces, unverifiable sources.* Because there are no objective guidelines in place to verify their accuracy, the vast majority of Internet sources (including Wikipedia) fall under the category of unacceptable sources for academic research. Consult with your instructor if you would like to request an exception to this rule. You should also avoid using certain texts in your school or public library as secondary sources, including fiction (suitable as a subject, but not as a research reference), editorial writing, and some work written before the current standards for academic writing were put into place. Consult with your instructor before using any source written before 1980.

The MLA Works-Cited List

As you compile your working bibliography, you should record each source according to the documentation format of the MLA works-cited list, or bibliography, which you will be required to include at the end of your research paper. The summary below includes the most common sources; a full listing can be found in the *MLA Handbook for Writers of Research Papers*, seventh edition, by Joseph Gibaldi (New York: Modern Language Association, 2009), in your library. Works-cited lists should be double-spaced and begin on a new page, each entry should be given a hanging indent of one-half inch, and you should put a single space after all punctuation. The first author's name is always listed last name first; the list should be alphabetized according to the author's last name. If the work is anonymous, alphabetize according to the first significant word of the title ("The Brooklyn Bridge" would go under "B" not "T"). See Appendix A for more information about citing sources.

Plagiarism and How to Avoid It

Plagiarism is the use of someone else's work—words, ideas, or illustrations; published or unpublished—without giving the creator of that work sufficient credit. A serious breach of scholarly ethics, plagiarism can have serious consequences. Students risk a failing grade or disciplinary action ranging from suspension to expulsion. A record of such action can adversely affect professional opportunities in the future as well as graduate school admission. For details regarding plagiarism and how to avoid it, see Appendix B, p. 67.

WRITER'S **CHECKLIST**
Processing Research Sources

- *Selection.* Read through the sources quickly to determine whether they will be of any use.
- *Critical reading.* Read carefully all sources that pass the first cut, taking notes about anything related to your topic.
- *Documentation.* Always record the full bibliographical information of any source you consult, in case you end up citing it in your paper, and always record its location in the library or on the Internet, so that you can find it again if you need to.
- *Notetaking.* Once you have decided a source will be part of your paper, think about it critically: read it, reflect on it, and write about it. For a research paper, critical thinking will mean taking notes. It is imperative that you write down everything you might need for your paper, even for electronic sources. The more work you put into the note-taking stage, the more work you will save yourself when it comes time to write. When taking notes:

- Summarize the entire text. These summaries will help keep you organized and you will be able to use them for your annotated bibliography.
- Copy quotations *only* when there is a crucial idea or formulation that you know you will cite verbatim in your paper.
- Be sure that you copy exactly what is in the text, mark it with quotation marks, and record the page numbers where it occurs.
- Write down the rest of the material that you will need as paraphrase, translating the source's words and arguments into your own.
- Always note the page number(s) to which your paraphrase corresponds, since you will need to document material you have paraphrased.
- Use paraphrasing as the first step toward incorporating the information and arguments of others into the argument and structure of your own paper.
- *Summarizing.* Summarize each source as an entry in your annotated bibliography, a particular form of summary used to organize and present your research before you actually sit down to write your own paper.
- Provide the full bibliographical reference as the title of each entry, in MLA style unless otherwise specified by your instructor (see Appendix A for a guide to MLA style).
- Make each entry a substantial single-spaced paragraph, usually between half a page and a page long.
- Summarize the part of the book or article that is relevant to your research in the same way as you learned to summarize an essay, beginning your summary with a statement of the text's argument. Sometimes your entry will summarize the entire text, sometimes only a part of it.
- Conclude each entry by evaluating the source in terms of its applicability to your topic and outlining your next step in working with the source.
- Bear in mind the following questions in preparing the entries of an annotated bibliography:
  - In what ways has this source altered my sense of where my paper is going?
  - What new ideas or approaches to my topic has it introduced?
  - What gaps in my knowledge of the topic has it filled in?
  - In what ways (if any) was it insufficient, and what questions (if any) did it leave unanswered?
  - What research still remains for me to do?

Summarizing Your Sources in the Annotated Bibliography

In addition to helping you organize your sources and refine your paper topic, a well-executed annotated bibliography can also provide the backbone of the research paper itself. After all, you will also need to summarize other people's arguments in the body of the paper. Moreover, if you can clarify the relationship between your argument and theirs, you will be well on the way to an original thesis. Your instructor will have specific instructions for the bibliography, including number of sources, type of source, and the form of each entry. Pay close attention to these instructions. Here is one of the entries from Amanda's annotated bibliography of three sources for her five- to seven-page research paper on missionaries in Igboland.

Wallace 1

Amanda Wallace
Professor Pike
Introduction to World Literature
19 February 2011

Annotated Bibliography – Source #1

Bastian, Misty L. "Young Converts: Christian Missions, Gender and Youth in Onitsha, Nigeria 1880–1929." *Anthropological Quarterly* 73.3 (Jul. 2000): 145–58. *JSTOR.* Web. 4 Nov. 2011. This article studies the activities of Church Missionary Society (Anglican) missionaries in Igboland in southeastern Nigeria during the end of the 19th century and the beginning of the 20th century. The article particularly focuses on the education of Igbo women. Bastian argues the "body/mind disciplines" helped to form a new category of identity among Igbo people known as "*ndi kris,* the Christian people" (145). The article provides historical information about the missionaries, many of them children of former slaves, and argues that their first success came when they offered education in "number literacy" and in reading and writing in English along with Christian teachings. As some Christian Igbo became wealthy and powerful, more girls were brought to these schools to help them marry into these families. Many of these were cut off from traditional customs and identities, which caused conflict. Young men and women adopted modern clothing and customs through

Every entry should begin with its source, in MLA format.

Begin the entry with a general sentence summarizing the source.

Summarize the argument of the source in a few sentences.

Avoid quotes from your source of more than a few words. Try to paraphrase and summarize information in your own language.

Wallace 2

this education and hoped to find jobs or marriage prospects in the colonial administration. For young people, the effect was both liberating and constricting. Although I am not writing about girls and women in particular, Bastian's article will help me understand the background of Michael Obi and his wife, who would have been educated in schools like the ones Bastian describes. It is clearly written and its research based on the same area that "Dead Men's Path" is set in. She suggests some reasons for the conflict between old and new in the story. What I don't know yet is how different the situation when Obi is taking over the school in 1949 is from the situation Bastian describes in the 1920s when he would have been in school.

Once you have summarized the source, evaluate its usefulness for your own project.

Conclude with any questions the source raises or new sources it suggests you need to seek out.

7

WRITING A
RESEARCH PAPER

Once you have completed your research and summarized each source you will be using in your annotated bibliography (see Chapter 6), you will have probably formulated at least a provisional argument for your topic. Now is the time to formalize that argument and generate a thesis for your paper.

WRITER'S CHECKLIST
Generating an Argument and a Thesis

- *Reconsider initial assumptions.* You have probably begun your research with a set of expectations about your topic. In what way has your new research caused you to revise or refine your initial assumptions to account for new or different information or interpretations? The gap between your expectations and your results is fertile ground for generating a thesis.
- *Review and compare facts and analysis.* Consider ways to organize and bring together the information and analysis you have assembled from your different sources. Are there still gaps in your knowledge that will need to be filled in with further research? Look for a new source that can supplement what you already know. Make lists or an idea map to help organize your questioning process.
- *Review and compare arguments.* For each entry of your annotated bibliography, you summarized the argument of your source. Which aspects of each argument are persuasive? Which are not? Do all your sources agree about the topic? Points of disagreement can often provide a focus for your own argument.
- *Review and compare evaluations.* For each entry of your annotated bibliography, you evaluated your source. Now consider how your evaluation of each source affects the way you will use its information and argument.
- *Look back at your work.* Now that you are familiar with a body of knowledge about your topic, do you have a sense of what you want to say about it? If you don't yet, try reading another source to gain a different perspective.

> • *Identify a clear goal for your research paper argument.* Seek the most effective way to organize your materials and to guide your reader through a comprehensive but pointed presentation of a specific topic. As opposed to a court case, a research paper will persuade your reader most effectively by addressing all aspects of the topic, not just the ones that support your own views, and by including different perspectives on each issue you raise.

Making an Outline

Having chosen the factual and historical material she needed to support her argument, and reviewed her analysis paper for the arguments she wanted to make about "Dead Men's Path," Amanda outlined her paper. There are many styles of outline, from very broad to extremely detailed. Aim for something in between, as Amanda did in hers:

Missionaries in Igboland:
The Background of "Dead Men's Path"—An Outline

1. Opening paragraph: the background of "Dead Men's Path"
   1.1. Summary of historical sources
   1.2. Thesis: Being a Christian in Igboland offered positive new possibilities for some people but also cut them off from important traditions.
2. Body of paper
   2.1. The history of Christian missions in Igboland in the late 19th and early 20th centuries
      2.1.1. Historical background – taking in of outcasts
      2.1.2. Historical background – offer of education, wealth, status
      2.1.3. How it is reflected in the story
   2.2. The Igbo response to the missions and the "modern ways"
      2.2.1. Historical background – Igbo tendency toward dialogue
      2.2.2. Reflected in story – Balogun argues neither headmaster nor priest lives up to his position
   2.3. Interpretation of the story – the image of the path in terms of this conflict
3. Conclusion – the path and the garden as a glimpse of resolution of conflict
4. Works Cited

Writing the First Draft

The more accomplished your first draft is, the better your revisions will be, and the less work you will have in making those revisions. Here are some tips for producing a strong first draft:

- *Take advantage of your outline.*
  - ○ *Do* use the outline to keep yourself on track and organize your material.
  - ○ *Don't* follow it blindly: if you don't like how the paper is unfolding, revise your outline.
- *Use your annotated bibliography as your starting point.*
  - ○ *Do* incorporate the analysis and language from your bibliography into your own argument in the final paper, but;
  - ○ *Don't* just copy the argument of each source into your own paper.
- *Be selective in using your research.*
  - ○ *Do* let your thesis dictate a logical sequence of argumentation and guide how you assemble your notes.
  - ○ *Don't* include research and notes simply because you have done them or you like them.
- *Be selective in choosing quotations.* Never take a quotation for granted.
  - ○ *Do* make sure your analysis of each quote is at least as long as the quote.
  - ○ *Don't* include long quotes without incorporating them into your argument with your own analysis.
  - ○ *Do* use the quote as evidence to support the argument made in your analysis.
  - ○ *Don't* use quotes as arguments on their own.
  - ○ *Do* summarize or paraphrase the information that you want to incorporate into your own argument, followed by proper documentation.
  - ○ *Don't* use quotes to provide factual information; quote a secondary source only if you are going to analyze an argument it contains, and a primary source only if you are going to perform a textual analysis.

For rules regarding MLA in-text citations and the works-cited list, see Appendix A (p. 57).

Revising

Your instructor may require you to hand in one or more drafts before the final version of the research paper is due, or he or she may leave the number of drafts you write to your own discretion. No paper will be acceptable without at least one round of revisions however, so you should budget your time accordingly. Be sure also to allow time for someone else to read your first draft, whether your instructor, a writing center tutor, a friend or relative, or all of the above. Here is a checklist for troubleshooting an initial draft:

- *Find and clarify your thesis.* Sometimes you will have begun writing without having fully clarified your thesis to yourself; other times, the process of writing may have led you to modify your thesis.
  - *Look in the conclusion.* This is where you will often discover that you have actually formulated what your paper is about.
  - *Analyze each paragraph.* What is the argument? How is it related to what came before and to what comes next?
- *Get the page count right.* Many first drafts are either too short or too long.
  - Do not include the title page and the Works Cited page in your page count.
  - Do not think that you will fool anyone by increasing or shrinking your font or margins.
  - Do not count a paper that runs a couple of lines onto the fifth page as a five-page paper.
- *Lengthen your paper the right way.* Amanda's initial draft for a five- to seven-page paper was just over four pages, and she used these strategies to produce a stronger, and longer, second paper:
  - Expand the analysis of your examples.
  - Spell out your argument; many early drafts assume the argument is self-evident when it is not.
  - Introduce additional evidence in support of your argument.
- *Shorten your paper the right way.* If your initial draft is already overlong, remember that revision is bound to add to that length. Here are some strategies to trim the fat as you add in the meat:
  - Find redundant examples and delete or shorten overly long quotations. Read through your paper, asking of every exam-

ple and every quotation: What is it doing here? How does it relate to my thesis? How does it provide support to my argument? If you can't answer these questions, delete the example and the quotation.

○ Keep a sharp eye out for repetition. Seldom do you need to say anything twice in a paper.

○ *Get help.* All of the strategies above will be more effective if you do them with the assistance of your instructor, the Writing Center, a classmate, or a friend.

• *Remedy* all mechanical errors that you didn't catch the first time around—mistakes of grammar, awkward or improper diction, misspellings of words, problems of citation or documentation.

○ *Refer* to Tips for Avoiding Common Paper-Writing Errors in Chapter 5 (p. 24).

○ *Be proactive.* Often, your instructor will simply circle or high-light mechanical mistakes and you will be required to figure out what is wrong and fix it. If you are not sure what the problem is, be sure to ask your instructor or a writing center tutor.

Because there is not space to include more than one draft of Amanda's research paper, we have included a later version, while indicating in the notes some of the revisions she made along the way.

Wallace 1

Amanda Wallace
Professor Pike
Introduction to World Literature
30 March 2011

Missionaries in Igboland:
What's at the End of the Dead Men's Path?

When Anglican missionaries came to Igboland in southeastern Nigeria in the middle of the 19th century, they did not just bring a new religion. They also brought the promise of education and social advance to this region of Nigeria. In Chinua Achebe's short story "Dead Men's Path," written in the 1950s, old ways and new ways are at the center of the conflict between the new headmaster, Michael Obi, and his wife and the village

Wallace 2

priest and many villagers regarding a path that runs through the school ground. However, it is not clear from the story whose side we should take. Neither side is completely sympathetic and neither side is completely wrong. The difficulty to take a side in Achebe's story reflects the difficult choices facing Igbo people during the first half of the 20th century (the story takes place in 1949). Being a Christian and adopting the modern ways of the colonizers meant going to school, getting a job, gaining wealth, and being part of the modern world. But it also meant giving up traditional beliefs, ties to the community, and even one's own family.

The thesis relates ambiguity in the story to ambiguity in the history that Amanda researched.

Here, Amanda outlines the main argument structuring the historical material.

Missionaries from the Anglican Church Missionary Society made their first mission in Igboland in Onitsha, on the Niger River, in the 1860s (Isichei 211). This is also near the setting of "Dead Men's Path," since Nancy Obi mentions her belief that outdated teachers should be traders in the Onitsha market (Achebe 44). Some of these missionaries were children of freed slaves who had returned to Africa and some were Europeans (Bastian 145). One of the most effective ways the missionaries had to convert the Igbo to Christianity was to offer them education in reading and writing in English and in math (146). Bastian writes that by the early 20th century a new "category of identity," or group of people, had come into being, known as "*ndi kris*, the Christian people" (146). Some of these people, like twins, would have been outcasts in traditional Igbo practice (146). This means that the new ways would have offered opportunities that these people might not have had under the old ways. It also means traditional Igbo might have been suspicious of the missionaries. For example, some were suspected of practicing witchcraft because of their interest in outcasts and their different beliefs and religious practices (146).

If your quote introduces an unfamiliar or difficult term, make sure that you briefly explain that term to show that you know what it means.

There were other reasons to be interested in the missionaries besides their taking in outcasts. Although some

Try to make your topic sentences provide a transition ("outcasts") from the previous paragraph as well as summarize the argument of the current paragraph.

Wallace 3

elders were suspicious, many Igbo were excited about the possibility of learning English (147). Some, as Elizabeth Isichei writes, saw a mission as a status symbol for a community or a way of gaining economic prosperity (211). Some people of Onitsha, Bastian argues, thought it would be useful to have young men who knew English and the ways of the outsiders but were loyal to the local ruler (147). Some ndi kris became wealthy and powerful men, making it seem attractive to follow them and making families desire to educate their daughters to marry them, or for their fiancés to pay for their education, as they wanted to have Christian and modern wives:

> Young Christian men with an eye to advancement within the CMS [Christian Missionary Society] and colonial administrative hierarchy were already becoming convinced at this early period of the need for Christian, relatively sophisticated wives who could offer domestic support to their husbands in a manner approved by the Europeans. Such wives were considered by men a token of youthful male success within the emerging colonial class structure and were, indeed, an integral part of the development of an elite, Christian class. (Bastian 148)

This is the situation of Michael Obi and his wife at the start of "Dead Men's Path," when he is appointed by the "Mission authorities" as "headmaster of the Ndume Central School in January 1949" (Achebe 44). They have been married two years, both have embraced "modern methods" (44) and both are ambitious.

The Obis are also very worried about their place in what Bastian terms the "colonial class structure" in the quote above. The conflict over the path comes because they are worried what the "Government Education Officer" might think on his upcoming inspection. Obi worries that, "The villagers might, for all I know, decide to use the schoolroom for a pagan ritual during the inspec-

---

If the author of the text cited is clear or already in the sentence, you don't need to put it in the in-text citation.

Separate quotes of more than four lines as a block, indented one inch and double-spaced. Do not use open and closing quotation marks. Place in square brackets any explanatory material that you add to the quote.

Always remind the reader about why the information you have presented is important. Here, it relates to information in the story.

In this paragraph, Amanda uses the historical material she has presented to help interpret character motivation within the story.

Wallace 4

tion" (Achebe 45). Although it is assumed that both Mike and Nancy have been educated in CMS schools and that they are practicing Christians, we never hear anything about their faith or religious beliefs. In the way the narrator presents their characters, they are concerned about being modern not about being good Christians. Obi is worried the Government Education Officer will think that he is tolerating beliefs that it is the school's "whole purpose ... to eradicate" (45). His wife's aim to make a "dream garden" with "a marigold flowerbed and the hedges" (45) tells us that she wants the school to look like she imagines an English school to look and not the way an Igbo village would look traditionally.

The way Isichei describes it, the missionaries succeeded in their goals "not through dialogue with adults, but by cutting children off from their traditional culture and placing them in the artificially unanimous environment of the school" (212). This strategy is related to the battle over the path in the story, since the "young headmaster" cuts off the path by planting "heavy sticks" where it enters and leaves the compound and by adding "barbed wire" (Achebe 45). In contrast, the village priest first attempts to have a dialogue with Obi, citing the proverb, "What I always say is: let the hawk perch and let the eagle perch" (45). This proverb is consistent with Isichei, who writes that, "The Igbo response which is given most often in mission records was to state that all religions worship the same God, and that the particular forms they take are those appropriate for Igboland, and Christianity was suitable for both black and white Europeans" (214). Diane Akers Rhoads also argues that, "The Igbos as a whole reveal themselves more tolerant of other cultures than the Europeans, who merely see the Igbos as uncivilized" (63). The "old man" in the story demonstrates this difference, as he comes to see the "young headmaster" and tries to have a dialogue.

Here, Amanda moves to the next section of the body of the paper in her outline: the reaction of traditional Igbo to the missionaries and "modern ways."

Wallace 5

Things have changed by the end of the story, once the diviner orders "heavy sacrifices to propitiate ancestors insulted by the fence" (46), because the villagers give up the idea of dialogue and instead violently reopen the path. According to Fidelis Odun Balogun, "the priest fails to live up to the wisdom in the proverb he quotes," which is "that the idea of compromise in settling crisis is entrenched in the tradition" (71). For Balogun, neither Obi nor the village priest is a worthy representative of the position they represent, since Obi is "misguided and superficial in his conception of modernity" (70). Isichei argues that, "Today most Igbo have been baptized, and traditional religion is the preserve of a small ageing minority. But the missionary victory is only apparent," since many Christian Igbo tend toward "syncretism," or a combination of religions, or to "secularism," the rejection of both (212). Still, for Isichei, the missionary's attitude generally reflected Obi's behavior, because it "tended to proceed by assertion, rather than by argument" (213). In contrast, Balogun imagines a modern authority that would be more diplomatic and have the "humility and wisdom produced by a good education" (74), and he also does not dismiss Obi's suggestion of a detour for the path as impossible to consider (70). The critics don't agree about how we should evaluate the characters and their positions, but they do agree that by the end of the story there is absolute division between them.

Both characters seem wrong in their behavior. Obi is wrong because he mocks the beliefs of the villagers and because he uses his authority just because he can to block the path. The village priest is wrong, as Balogun says, because he doesn't follow his own saying. That is why there is violent conflict by the end of the story. The young headmaster starts it with his barbed wire, but the priest makes it worse by not just opening up the path, but also "trampl[ing] to death" the flowers and even "pull[ing] down" a school building (46). And both char-

Wallace 6

acters suffer. The villagers, surely, will not get their path back now that they have attacked the school, and the headmaster is considered to have shown "misplaced zeal" by the "white Supervisor" whose visit he was worried so much about. What's more, because the report thinks there is a "tribal war situation developing between the school and the village" (46), the village is likely to be closely watched by the authorities, and will probably suffer in all sorts of ways from it.

For Balogun, both characters show an "incongruity between [their] beliefs (traditional or Christian) and actual reality" (82). Obi's belief in "modern methods" and the priest's belief in tradition create a crisis because they don't also look at the situation in front of them. I agree with Balogun, but I think there is another way to understand the story. Achebe calls the story "Dead Men's Path." Why? It could be because it is a thing of the past that is getting in the way of the future. That's how the young headmaster sees it, but it's hard to sympathize very much with the young headmaster. It could be because the ancestors still need to use the "ancestral footpath" or disaster will happen, like the village priest says (Achebe 45). According to Balogun, the critic Robert Wren interprets the story as siding with the priest (70). But I agree with Balogun that the priest is not completely right either. Perhaps the title refers to both of these positions.

If we know about the history of missionary schools in Igboland and the mixed feelings that the Igbo people had about them, it makes sense that neither side would be completely sympathetic. Like the history itself, the story shows that there are good arguments on both sides and it shows that there are bad arguers on both sides. The fact that we don't see a single sensible person in the story seems to be Achebe's way of telling us that most of the time things did not go well when colonizers came to places like Igboland. But the story is not completely hopeless, and

Here the paper shifts into the final section of the paper body in the outline: the analysis of the story in light of the historical research.

Don't be afraid to disagree with critics, as long as you have strong evidence to back up your argument.

Wallace 7

this is another reason Achebe might have decided to make neither side win the argument. The path is not just there to stand for what Obi believes and what the priest believes. It is also an important image in the story because it brings together both sides, the school and the village, the old and the new.

The presence of the path within the grounds of the school suggests that the school has not been completely "cut off" from the past that the Igbo believe the path still leads to. This suggests that the school itself has some kind of role to play in the life of the village. In order for the old ways to somehow coexist with the new, the path must be allowed somehow to continue to pass through the school. Otherwise the old and the new will be cut off from each other, and there will be destruction in the village.

In this way, the dead men's path in this story works as an image of the conflict between old and new ways, and Igbo traditions and missionaries' teachings. But it also suggests that it could be possible to resolve those conflicts. The difficulty of resolving seems to have something to do with the garden. It is because of the garden that Mike and Nancy notice the path and to protect the garden from figures such as the "old woman" walking "through a marigold flowerbed" (45) that the fence is built. And it is the garden that suffers the full force of the anger of the villagers. Like the path, the garden is an image of nature, "a place of beauty" and life (45) but carefully tended and needing protection. Almost invisible, the dead man's path is like a ghost haunting the school. But it is also a ghost that helps to lead children into the world, just as the school, in a way, also does. It is as if Achebe sees both ways as necessary, but cannot yet see how they can perch together in the same space, like the hawk and the eagle.

In her conclusion, Amanda turned out to be able to return to the conclusion of her analysis paper, but with a completely new context provided by her research.

Wallace 8

Works Cited

Achebe, Chinua. "Dead Men's Path." Ed. David L. Pike and Ana M. Acosta. *Literature: A World of Writing.* New York: Pearson Longman, 2011. 44–46. Print.

Balogun, Fidelis Odun. *Tradition and Modernity in the African Short Story: An Introduction to a Literature in Search of Critics.* New York: Greenwood, 1991. Print.

Bastian, Misty L. "Young Converts: Christian Missions, Gender and Youth in Onitsha, Nigeria 1880–1929." *Anthropological Quarterly* 73.3 (Jul. 2000): 145–58. *JSTOR.* Web. 4 Mar. 2011.

Isichei, Elizabeth. "Seven Varieties of Ambiguity: Some Patterns of IGBO Response to Christian Missions." *Journal of Religion in Africa* 3.2 (1970): 209–27. *JSTOR.* Web. 4 Mar. 2011.

Rhoads, Diana Akers. "Culture in Chinua Achebe's *Things Fall Apart.*" *African Studies Review* 36.2 (Sept. 1993): 61–72. *JSTOR.* Web. 4 Mar. 2011.

The works-cited list contains an entry for every text cited in the body of the paper.

8

TAKING
AN EXAM

In addition to the types of writing discussed in the previous chapters, you are also likely to be asked to do graded writing in an exam setting. Part of these exams will be simple factual answers, either a brief sentence or two or multiple choice, similar in format to the periodic quizzes you also may be given. In addition to testing your knowledge base, you may also be asked to write essay questions as part of your exam. The two most common are (1) passage identifications, in which you are given a series of passages from different assigned texts that you must identify correctly and analyze; and (2) a thematic essay, in which you are asked to write about a certain topic in relation to two or more different literary texts. The first of these assignments is closely related to the literary analysis paper and the second to the comparison paper (both of these are discussed in Chapter 5).

The Passage Identification

Here is a typical prompt for a passage identification on an exam, along with a sample passage:

For each passage:

  1) Identify the title, author (where appropriate), and speaker (where appropriate) of the work to which it belongs, and **briefly** situate the passage within the context of the work as a whole. (5 points)

2) Analyze the language and imagery of the passage. How does the way the passage is written contribute to our understanding of it? What form does it take (image, simile, metaphor) and what is its function in the passage? In what ways does it relate to any main theme or themes of the work? Does it reinforce the theme, alter its meaning, or both at once? (35 points)

I **do not** expect lengthy essays, but I **do** expect a substantial discussion of each passage, concise but long enough to make a coherent argument with **specific examples** based on the language and imagery in each passage. **Avoid**: plot summary, sweeping generalizations ("as with all Greek tragedies"), platitudes ("In *The Odyssey* true love wins out in the end"), and nondescriptive adjectives ("brilliant," "great").

Passage (4)

"Mankind is deceptive, and will deceive you.
Come, bake loaves for him and keep setting them by his head
And draw on the wall each day that he lay down."
She baked his loaves and placed them by his head
and marked on the wall the day that he lay down.
The first loaf was desiccated,
the second stale, the third moist, the fourth turned white,...
the fifth sprouted gray mold, the sixth is still fresh.
The seventh—suddenly he touched him and the man awoke.

Here are some strategies for responding to the prompt: the first thing you need to know to answer a passage identification question, naturally, is the names and authors of all of the texts you are responsible for having read in your class. If you have read carefully, taken notes, and listened and contributed to class discussions, you will not likely have any problem distinguishing one passage from the other. A good studying tool for these questions is the "Making Comparisons" box on p. 21. Use this box while you are reading each text, and you will be in good shape; use it again while you are studying, and you will have no trouble identifying most passages.

The second part of the prompt above asks you to analyze the language and imagery of the passage. This is to test the degree to which you have mastered the skill of literary analysis (see Chapter 5). The only difference in doing a literary analysis in a passage identification is the constraint of space and time. You must be selective in what you choose to write and you must be concise in the way you express yourself. Do not try to cover everything in a passage. As the prompt puts it: make a coherent argument that addresses the most important imagery in the passage. Be sure to relate that argument to a theme of the text as a whole.

There are many elements you could choose to discuss in the passage given, which is near the end of *The Epic of Gilgamesh*, when Utanapishtim asks his wife to bake one loaf of bread for every day Gilgamesh sleeps, in order to prove to the hero that he has lost the wager that he, like a true immortal, could go without sleep. The explicit point of the passage is that the loaves of bread provide a physical demonstration of the passage of time. You cannot fake the time it takes for bread to pass through the stages of its decomposition, which the passage details with evident pleasure: from freshness, to varying degrees of mold through "desiccation," the return of the bread to dust. Bread itself is a powerful image of life, the basic food of mortals as well as a sacramental food in many religions, including Christianity. But it is also a reminder to Gilgamesh of his own mortality and of the loss of his companion Enkidu, especially since it is in response to Enkidu's death (and graphically depicted decomposition) that Gilgamesh has made his quest to Utanapishtim to discover the secret of eternal life. Like the bread, and like Enkidu, he too will eventually die, decay, and dry up. In the desert world of *Gilgamesh*, dust is the basic element. Men are created from dust and when they die, like the loaf of bread, they return to it. Faced with the truth of these loaves of bread, Gilgamesh must realize the truth about his own mortality, which he has been fleeing for much of the poem.

Few instructors would expect to hear so much about this passage, but note that all of the analysis derives from the imagery available in it, and from the associations it has with the rest of the poem. It is available to any reader who has worked carefully with the language of the text.

The Thematic Essay

Here is a sample prompt for a thematic essay question:

Comparative Essay. 50 minutes. Compose an essay on one of the two topics below comparing several texts from the semester's readings. Be sure to define the way(s) in which you will understand the terms and/or themes discussed in your essay. Provide a clear thesis, organize your essay carefully in terms of your overall argument, and provide PARTICULAR AND DETAILED EXAMPLES from each work chosen in order to support or test your thesis. Focus on theme, imagery, and motifs rather than on plot events. Include at least one text from the first half and at least one text from the second half of the semester.

1. Throughout the semester, we have discussed ways in which texts refer to other texts, whether through an explicit (named) or an implicit (unnamed) allusion. In an essay, discuss the use of allusion in at least two texts read this semester. You may choose to discuss a single text and one or more texts which it cites and/or to which it alludes, a specific source text and the way several later texts cite and/or allude to it, or a specific type or form of allusion and the way it is used in several different texts. In all three options, be sure to be specific in your examples, and to consider the ways in which allusion is or is not faithful to the source text, and why.
2. The depiction of female characters has been a major theme of discussion throughout the semester. Write an essay selecting, in your opinion, the two most unusual female characters we have encountered. Make a case for each of your two selections in terms of the other characters from the semester. What makes each one "unusual"? Now, compare them: what similarities and differences are there between them? How do you account for these similarities and differences?

Even more than the passage identification resembles a literary analysis, a thematic essay is simply a form of comparison essay. The directions in the prompt are basically the same as the directions you would receive for writing any analytical paper: provide a clear thesis, organize your essay carefully in terms of your overall argument, and provide PARTICULAR AND DETAILED EXAMPLES from each work chosen in order to support or test your thesis. Focus on theme, imagery, and motifs rather than on plot events. The only difference—and it is a significant one—is that you are not given the question ahead of time, and must formulate your particular topic and thesis on the spot. In order to be prepared to do this, your preparation should include the following steps of review:

- Familiarize yourself with the "Making Comparisons" box on p. 21. This should be your rubric for preparing to answer any thematic question.
- Review your class notes. Your instructor will draw the prompts either explicitly or implicitly from topics that have been discussed in class, usually in the context of more than one text.
- Make a list of the topics that appear in reference to more than one text in your notes.
- Make a list of the texts that are relevant or that you are comfortable discussing in terms of each of these topics.
- Sketch out, either on your own, or with classmates (always study with classmates if you have the option) possible arguments relating each text to the topic and to other texts.
- Choose specific passages and examples from each text that seem relevant to these possible arguments.
- Even if the instructor surprises you with the specific topic, your preparation will have prepared you with a ready body of knowledge about each text in a variety of contexts. Using this body of knowledge, you will likely be able to formulate an essay in response to most topics your instructor will give you.

Appendix A

WORKING WITH MLA FORMATTING AND DOCUMENTATION

This appendix provides the basics of MLA formatting for the kinds of papers discussed in the prior chapters. It also provides information for documenting the most frequently encountered types of sources in the MLA Works Cited page.

Getting Started

Individual course directions may differ at times from MLA format, so when in doubt, follow the specific prompt for your assignment, or check with your instructor.

What kind of paper to use: *8½ by 11 inches, unlined, white paper*

What margins to use: Top, bottom, left, and right margins should all be one inch; unless instructed differently, *do not right-justify the page.*

Line spacing: *Double-space* all parts of your paper.

Page numbering: Number all pages in the top of the page. Type your name before the page number.

Title and heading: Unless told otherwise, *you do not need a title page* for your paper. Provide a heading with your name, your instructor's name, the title and number of the course, and the date in the top left margin of the first page. Type the title, centered on the next line. Begin the text of the page on the following line, at the left margin, indented five spaces or one-half inch:

Lanney 1

Rob Lanney

Ms. Franklin

English Composition 101

15 March 2011

Hamlet's Denmark

The setting of the court of Elsinore playes an important role in the action of Shakespeare's play. The historical Kronborg Castle, at Elsinore, in Denmark is the setting for the play. Critics like Hansen see

---

Works-cited list: Begin the works-cited list on a new page directly following the end of the body of the paper. If you have endnotes, the works-cited list should follow the endnotes on a new page.

- List the works in alphabetical order.
- Double-space within and between entries.
- Begin the first line of each entry on the left-hand margin. Indent any additional lines five spaces.
- Include in the list only works that you have cited in the paper.

Citing Sources in Your Essay

1. **Paraphrasing source material:** Place the author's name and the page number in parentheses. In the case of two authors, use "and" to join their names.

   Contrary to Hamlet's assumption that it is wholly corrupt, Elsinore has both the positive and the negative qualities of a royal court (Foakes 35).

2. **Using your own words with the author's name:** Place the page number in parentheses.

   Foakes argues that Hamlet believes the court to be corrupt, but the evidence of the play shows it in fact to have both positive and negative qualities (35).

3. **Quoting prose directly (less than five lines):** Use quotation marks and incorporate prose quotes of less than five lines into the text.

   According to Foakes, "The court of Elsinore . . . has a dual character" (35), or "The court of Elsinore . . . has a dual character" (Foakes 35).

4. **Quoting prose directly (five or more lines):** Separate passage from the main text as a block quotation by starting it on a new line and indenting the entire passage one inch. Introduce with a colon. *Do not use quotation marks around a block quotation.*

   Anthony Davies summarizes well the decision facing a filmmaker with regards to the setting of Elsinore:

   > The most immediate challenge to any filmmaker who approaches *Hamlet* is the treatment of Elsinore. The castle offers the major spatial opportunities of the play, and the film director has to decide whether Elsinore is essentially a place or a concept, and the extent to which it is subjectively or objectively seen. (20)

5. **Quoting poetry directly (less than three lines):** Place in quotation marks and incorporate into your own text. Mark line breaks with a forward slash (/) with a space on each side.

The nineteenth-century poet George Castle Rankin makes the "halls of Elsinore" a metaphor for Hamlet's troubled mind: "The puzzle vast and complicate / Which ravels all the world's affairs, / The maze of love and pride and hate" (56).

6. **Quoting poetry directly (three or more lines):**

The nineteenth-century poet George Castle Rankin makes the "halls of Elsinore" a metaphor for Hamlet's troubled mind:

> The puzzle vast and complicate
>   Which ravels all the world's affairs,
> The maze of love and pride and hate,
>   The conflict of beleaguering cares,
> All are unsolved as much as when
>   Thou hadst been wont to brood them o'er
> Wand'ring apart from gayer men
>   Among the halls of Elsinore. (56)

7. **Quoting drama directly:** When quoting dialogue between two or more characters, separate as a block quotation. Introduce each character's dialogue with the characters name, in block capitals, indented one inch from left margin, and followed by a period. Indent any lines that follow a further three spaces. If citing a play in verse, give act, scene, and line numbers in parentheses; if citing a play in prose, give page number in parentheses.

Hamlet and Horatio employ the shared location of Elsinore to connect the father's death with the mother's remarriage:

> HAMLET. But what is your affair in Elsinore?
>   We'll teach you to drink deep ere you depart.
> HORATIO. My lord, I came to see your father's funeral.
> HAMLET. I pray thee, do not mock me, fellow-student;
>   I think it was to see my mother's wedding. (1.2.174–78)

Documenting Sources in the MLA Works-Cited List

We provide the examples for the sources you are most likely to need to document. If you encounter a source that does not fall into any of the categories below, you will need to consult a more comprehensive guide, such as Joseph Gibaldi's *MLA Handbook for Writers of Research Papers*, seventh edition, published by the Modern Language Association of America, 2009.

Books

1. A book with one author:

Davies, Anthony. *Filming Shakespeare's Plays: The Adaptations of Laurence Olivier, Orson Welles, Peter Brook, Akira Kurosawa*. New York: Cambridge UP, 1988. Print.

2. Two or more books by the same author; list in alphabetical order by title:

Greenblatt, Stephen. *Hamlet in Purgatory*. Princeton: Princeton UP, 2001. Print.

— — —. *Will in the World: How Shakespeare Became Shakespeare*. New York: Norton, 2004. Print.

3. A book with two authors:

Gallagher, Catherine, and Stephen Greenblatt. *Practicing New Historicism*. Chicago: U of Chicago P, 2000. Print.

4. A book with an editor and no author:

Aasand, Hardin L., ed. *Stage directions in Hamlet: New Essays and New Directions*. Madison, N.J.: Fairleigh Dickinson UP, 2003. Print.

5. A book with two editors and no author:

Keller, James R., and Leslie Stratyner, eds. *Almost Shakespeare: Reinventing His Works for Cinema and Television*. Jefferson, NC: McFarland, 2004. Print.

6. A republished book:

Van Doren, Mark. *Shakespeare*. 1939. New York: New York Review Books Classics, 2005. Print.

7. A multivolume work:

Andrews, John F., ed. *William Shakespeare: His World, His Work, His Influence*. 3 vols. New York: Scribner, 1985. Print.

8. A translation:

Bonnefoy, Yves. *Shakespeare and the French Poet*. Trans. John Naughton. Chicago: U of Chicago P, 2004. Print.

9. A selection from an anthology or a collection:

Bertoldi, Andreas. "Shakespeare, Psychoanalysis, and the Colonial Encounter: The Case of Wulf Sachs's *Black Hamlet.*" *Postcolonial Shakespeares.* Ed. Ania Loomba and Martin Orkin. New York: Routledge, 1998. 235–58. Print.

Foakes, R. A. "Hamlet and the Court of Elsinore." *Shakespeare Survey 9: Hamlet.* Ed. Allardyce Nicoll. 1956. Cambridge: Cambridge UP, 2002. 35–44. Print.

10. A book with a corporate author:

Encyclopædia Britannica. *Shakespeare: The Essential Guide to the Life and Works of the Bard.* Hoboken, N.J.: John Wiley & Sons, 2007. Print.

11. A book in a series:

McEvoy, Sean, ed. *William Shakespeare's Hamlet: A Sourcebook.* Routledge Guides to Literature. New York: Routledge, 2006. Print.

12. An introduction, preface, forward, or afterword:

Naughton, John. Introduction. *Shakespeare and the French Poet.* Trans. and ed. John Naughton. Chicago: U of Chicago P, 2004. vii–xviii. Print.

13. A signed article in a reference work:

Kutscher, E. Y. "Aramaic." *Encyclopaedia Judaica.* 1st edition. 1972. Print.

14. An unsigned article in a reference work:

"Denmark." *Encylopœdia Britannica.* 15th edition. 1992. Print.

Periodicals

15. An article from a periodical paginated continuously through the annual volume:

Floyd-Wilson, Mary. "Ophelia and Femininity in the Eighteenth Century: 'Dangerous conjectures in ill-breeding minds.'" *Women's Studies* 21 (1992): 397–409. Print.

16. An article from a periodical paginated by issue:

Sanchez, Reuben. "'Thou com'st in such a questionable shape': Interpreting the Textual and Contextual Ghost in *Hamlet.*" *Hamlet Studies* 18.1–2 (1996): 65–84. Print.

17. A monthly periodical:

Bethell, Tom. "The Case for Oxford." *Atlantic Monthly* Oct. 1991: 45–61. Print.

18. A signed article in a weekly periodical:

Rosenbaum, Ron. "Shakespeare in Rewrite: After Four Hundred Years, Scholars Want to Change the Way We Read *Hamlet.*" *New Yorker* 13 May 2002: 68–77. Print.

19. A signed article in a daily newspaper (include section of paper with page number):

Hesse, Monica. "It's Hannah Again. Should We Take This?" *Washington Post* 1 Aug. 2008: C1. Print.

20. A signed review, letter to the editor, or editorial:

Thomson, David. "I Act, Therefore I Am." Rev. of *Olivier*, by Terry Coleman. *Nation* 5 Dec. 2004: 30–34. Print.

Samuelson, Robert J. "The Ownership Obsession." Editorial. *Washington Post* 30 Jul. 2008: A15. Print.

Glitzenstein, Eric. "Valuing Animals Doesn't Devalue Us." Letter. *Washington Post* 1 Aug. 2008: A16. Print.

Internet and Other Electronic Sources

21. An entire Internet site for an online scholarly project or database:

An International Database of Shakespeare on Film, Television and Radio. Ed. Murray Weston et al. British Universities Film and Video Council. BUFVC, n.d. Web. 1 Aug. 2010.

22. A short work within a scholarly project:

Gray, Terry A. "A Shakespeare Timeline." *Mr. William Shakespeare and the Internet.* Terry A. Gray, 17 Jun. 2008. Web. 1 Aug. 2010.

23. A personal home page or professional site:

Leong, Virginia. *Hamlet Movie Links.* N.p., n.d. Web. 1 Aug. 2010. <http://www.geocities.com/Athens/Parthenon/6261/hamlet.html>.

24. An online book:

Shakespeare, William. *The First Folios and Early Quartos of William Shakespeare.* Electronic Text Center. University of Virginia Library, n.d. Web. 1 Aug. 2010.

25. A part of an online book:

Shakespeare, William. *Hamlet (1623 First Folio Edition). The First Folios and Early Quartos of William Shakespeare.* Electronic Text Center. University of Virginia Library, n.d. Web. 1 Aug. 2010.

26. An article in a scholarly journal from a database:

Worthen, W. B. "*Hamlet* at Ground Zero: The Wooster Group and the Archive of Performance." *Shakespeare Quarterly* 59.3 (2008): 303–22. *Project Muse.* Web. 29 Apr. 2010.

27. A signed article in an online newspaper or on a newswire:

Holden, Michael. "Man held over theft of rare Shakespeare folio." *Reuters.* Thomson Reuters, 11 Jul. 2008. Web. 1 Aug. 2010.

28. An article in an online magazine:

Rosenbaum, Ron. "Shakespeare in Rewrite: After Four Hundred Years, Scholar Want to Change the Way We Read *Hamlet.*" *New Yorker.* Conde Nast, 13 May 2002. Web. 1 Aug. 2010.

Other Print and Nonprint Sources

29. A dissertation (abstracted in *Dissertation Abstracts International*):

Swindall, Lindsey R. "*Hamlet* in the Cinema." Diss. U of Oklahoma, 2007. *DAI* 68.01 (July 2008). Web. 1 Aug. 2010.

30. A film:

Hamlet. Dir. Michael Almereyda. Perf. Ethan Hawke, Kyle MacLachlan, Sam Shephard, Bill Murray, Julia Stiles. Miramax, 2000. Film.

31. A recording of a TV program or film:

Hamlet, Prince of Denmark. Dir. Rodney Bennett. Perf. Derek Jacobi, Claire Bloom, Patrick Stewart. 1980. Ambrose Video, 2002. DVD.

32. An audio recording:

Thomas, Ambroise. *Hamlet*. Cond. Antonio de Almeida. Perf. Thomas Hampson, June Anderson, Samuel Ramey. EMI Classics, 1995. CD.

33. Visual art:

Millais, John Everett. *Ophelia*. 1852. Tate Britain, London.

Sample Works Cited Pages: see Chapter 7, p. 51 and also Chapter 5, p. 29.

Appendix B

PLAGIARISM AND HOW TO AVOID IT

Plagiarism is using someone else's work—words, ideas, or illustrations; published or unpublished—without giving the creator of that work sufficient credit. A serious breach of scholarly ethics, plagiarism can have severe consequences. Students risk a failing grade or disciplinary action ranging from suspension to expulsion. A record of such action can adversely affect professional opportunities in the future as well as graduate school admission.

Avoiding Unintentional Plagiarism

It can be difficult to tell when you have unintentionally plagiarized something. The legal doctrine of **fair use** allows writers to use a limited amount of another's work in their own papers and books. To make sure that they are not plagiarizing that work, however, writers need to take care to credit accurately and clearly the source for *every* use as detailed in previous chapters. To use documentation and avoid unintentionally plagiarizing from a source, you need to be sure that you

- identify sources and information that need to be documented.
- document sources in a works-cited list.
- use material gathered from sources: summary, paraphrase, quotation.
- create in-text references.
- use correct grammar and punctuation to blend quotations into a paper.

Identifying Sources and Information That Need to Be Documented

Whenever you use information from **outside sources**, you need to identify the source of that material. Virtually all the information you find in outside sources requires documentation. The one major exception to this guideline is that you do not have to document common knowledge. **Common knowledge** is widely known information about current events, famous people, geographical facts, or familiar history. However, when in doubt, the safest strategy is to provide documentation.

Is It Plagiarism? Test Yourself on In-Text References
Read the excerpt marked "Original Source." Can you spot the plagiarism in the examples that follow?

Original Source

Ma Rainey's Black Bottom is a disturbing look at the consequences of waiting, especially as it relates to the precarious lot of black musicians during the pre-Depression era. Although the play features a still shot in the lives of several members of Ma Rainey's 1920s band, it is also suggestive of the many and varied oppressive forces under which the entire African American population labored at that time. From education to employment, blacks got the smallest share of the American pie, while clinging to an often self-destructive ideology of tolerance. Through the actions and dialogue of three crucial characters—the blues singer Ma Rainey, her piano player Toledo, and her trumpet player Levee—, Wilson conveys the damage that prolonged periods of waiting have caused the Afro-American artist. (Shannon 135–36).

Works Cited entry:
Shannon, Sandra G. "The Long Wait: August Wilson's *Ma Rainey's Black Bottom*." *Black American Literature Forum* 25.1 (Spring 1991): 135–46. Print.

Plagiarism Example 1
One critic argues that *Ma Rainey's Black Bottom* is about the lives of black jazz artists before the Depression, but also **conveys the**

damage that prolonged periods of waiting have caused the Afro-American artist. This damage helps to suggest the different kind of **oppressive forces** against which the **entire Afro-American population labored at that time** (135–36).

> *What's wrong?* The source's name is not given, and there are no quotation marks around words taken directly from the source (in **boldface** in the example).

Plagiarism Example 2
Shannon argues that the plight of the musicians in Ma Rainey's band "is also suggestive of the many and varied oppressive forces under which the entire Afro-American population labored at that time." Wilson uses conflict within the band to make an argument about the lives of African Americans during the 1920s.

> *What's wrong?* **The page number of the source is missing.** Parenthetical references should immediately follow the material being quoted, paraphrased, or summarized. You may omit a parenthetical reference only if the information that you have included in your attribution is sufficient to identify the source in your works-cited list and no page number is needed.

Plagiarism Example 3
In many areas, blacks did not receive a fair **share of the American pie.** Three of the play's main characters—the lead singer Ma Rainey, **her piano player Toledo,** and the rebellious horn player Levee—, demonstrate how **prolonged periods of waiting** have harmed **the African American artist** (Shannon 135–36).

> *What's wrong?* A paraphrase should capture a specific idea from a source but must not duplicate the writer's phrases and words (in **boldface** in the example). In the example, the wording and sentence structure follow the source too closely.

Works Cited

Achebe, Chinua. "Dead Men's Path." Pike and Acosta 44–46.

— — —. "The African Writer and the English Language." Damrosch and Pike 850–55.

Alexie, Sherman. "This Is What It Means To Say Phoenix, Arizona." Pike and Acosta 519–25.

Bastian, Misty L. "Young Converts: Christian Missions, Gender and Youth in Onitsha, Nigeria 1880–1929." *Anthropological Quarterly* 73.3 (2000): 145–58. *JSTOR*. Web. 11 Mar. 2011.

Damrosch, David. *How to Read World Literature*. Malden, MA: Wiley-Blackwell, 2009. Print.

Damrosch, David, ed. *Teaching World Literature*. New York: Modern Language Association, 2009. Print.

Damrosch, David, and David L. Pike, eds. *The Longman Anthology of World Literature*. 2nd ed. Six vols. New York: Pearson, 2009. Print.

Frontain, Raymond-Jean. "Cosmos versus Empire: Teaching the *Ramayana* in a Comparative Setting." Ed. Damrosch 343–52.

Isichei, Elizabeth. "Seven Varieties of Ambiguity: Some Patterns of IGBO Response to Christian Missions." *Journal of Religion in Africa* 3.2 (1970): 209–27. *JSTOR*. Web. 11 Mar. 2011.

Pike, David L., and Ana M. Acosta. *Literature: A World of Writing*. New York: Pearson Longman, 2011. Print.

Venuti, Lawrence. "Teaching in Translation." Ed. Damrosch 86–96.

ADDITIONAL TITLES IN THE **WESSKA**
(WHAT EVERY STUDENT SHOULD KNOW ABOUT...) SERIES:

- *What Every Student Should Know About Avoiding Plagiarism* (ISBN 0-321-44689-5)

- *What Every Student Should Know About Citing Sources with APA Documentation* (ISBN 0-205-79581-1)

- *What Every Student Should Know About Citing Sources with MLA Documentation* (ISBN 0-205-71511-7)

- *What Every Student Should Know About Reading Maps, Figures, Photographs, and More* (ISBN 0-205-50543-0)

- *What Every Student Should Know About Using a Handbook* (ISBN 0-205-56384-8)

- *What Every Student Should Know About Writing Across the Curriculum* (ISBN 0-205-58913-8).

- *What Every Student Should Know About Creating Portfolios* (ISBN 0-205-57250-2)

- *What Every Student Should Know About Practicing Peer Review* (ISBN 0-321-44848-0)

- *What Every Student Should Know About Preparing Effective Oral Presentations* (ISBN 0-205-50545-7)

- *What Every Student Should Know About Study Skills* (ISBN 0-321-44736-0)

- *What Every Student Should Know About Procrastination* (ISBN 0-205-58211-7)